Of Men, Women and Witches

Of Men, Women and Witches

Stories from My Life

Jeyamohan

An English translation of *Uravidangal*

Translated from the Malayalam by
Sangeetha Puthiyedath

JUGGERNAUT BOOKS
C-I-128, First Floor, Sangam Vihar, Near Holi Chowk,
New Delhi 110080, India

First published by Juggernaut Books 2025
Originally published in Malayalam as *Uravidangal* by
Mathrubhumi Books 2011

10 9 8 7 6 5 4 3 2 1

P-ISBN: 978-93-5345-343-5
E-ISBN: 978-93-5345-844-7

Typeset in Adobe Caslon Pro by R. Ajith Kumar, Noida

Printed at Thomson Press India Ltd

For Achan,

ardent, fervent traveller–storyteller

Contents

Translator's Note

'Whatever is here, is found elsewhere, but what is not here is nowhere else,' asserts Vyasa unequivocally in the 'Adi Parva' of the Mahabharata. Had the epic poet been aware of Jeyamohan's memoir, he would have been more circumspect! Here is a work that brings to our mind what a twenty-year-old Franz Kafka wrote to his childhood friend Oskar Pollack:

> *I think we ought to read only the kind of books that wound or stab us. If the book we're reading doesn't wake us up with a blow to the head, what are we reading for? So that it will make us happy, as you write? … we need books that affect us like a disaster, that grieve us deeply, like the death of someone we loved more than ourselves, like being banished into forests far from everyone, like a suicide. A book must be the axe for the frozen sea within us. That is my belief.*

As we move through the pages of Jeyamohan's *Of Men, Women and Witches* (*Uravidangal*), we will be forced to remind ourselves that this is *not* a story; that the people we come across here *really* existed; that the events recounted here *really* happened. We come across a father who did not know how to love, whose unexpressed tenderness curdled within him, turned acidic and intolerably corrosive; a mother who lost her life swinging between inspiriting dreams and a nightmarish reality; a grandmother who, deprived of the larger-than-life canvas she felt she deserved, wasted her life in the *chakra vyuha* of legal cases. The father, the mother and the grandmother whom we meet in the pages of this book defy easy description. They sear into us as people who left a burning trail in life, and that of a boy who survived the house of lac to quietly tell the tale.

This is not Jeyamohan's life story. If we approach it as the record of a linear progression of a life from childhood to adulthood, as lineaments of a portrait of the artist as a young man, we are bound to be disappointed. Running through the chronicles is an implicit quest for meaning, for measure, for purpose and love. Here the lines that divide life and art blur. More than a story, what we encounter here are scalding slivers of memory that will smart long after the book is read and set aside. It is also the story of a land and a people who no longer exist and can no longer be recognized. Fragments shored against the ruins of a forgotten history – harsh, haunting and unquestionably moving.

I remember how deeply the book affected me when I read it years ago for the first time. At that time, I had no inkling that I would try my hand at translating it one day! Slowly it dawned on me that these vignettes could provide valuable clues – even keys – to understanding the writer and his writing. How can one translate such a text? At first, the task appeared too daunting.

Jeyamohan's language is a deft amalgam of precision and poetry. The symbolic and the concrete seamlessly fuse. However, there are times when his ruminations slide into what is suggestive and elliptical, revealing glimpses of a complex interiority caught in a maze-like reality. The adamantine parts were snatches of folk sayings and conversations in obscure regional dialects! How to capture their plain import, let alone their distinctive flavour?

It has been observed that the word 'translation' comes, etymologically, from the Latin for 'bearing across'. As a translator, one knows that even in the best instances a translation can only be an 'approximation' and not an exact reproduction, yet one forges ahead to bring forth what writers like Walter Benjamin and Alberto Manguel spelt out as its defining aspiration and objective. 'It is the task of the translator to release in his own language that pure language that is under the spell of another, to liberate the language imprisoned in a work in his re-creation of that work,' advocates Benjamin. And Manguel reminds us that, 'It is in the translation that the innocence lost after the first reading is restored under another guise, since the reader is once again faced with a new text and its attendant mystery. That is the inescapable paradox of translation, and also its wealth.'

Effective translation does not happen because a translator is familiar with two languages, but rather because the translator is able to touch, albeit briefly, the mind of the writer. Translating this slim volume – the original work is merely 142 pages long, took me almost two years to complete. The content was demanding and often emotionally taxing. But the most challenging aspect was the difficulty in finding words that captured the essential spirit of the text, not just the meaning. I attempted to overcome this by not overtly focusing on what is literal, but on the implicit meaning – that is, the spirit and the flavour of the original as much as I could. Sometimes even this was difficult for there were no accurate equivalent expressions in English for certain terms and words. In such cases, I retained the original word in Malayalam, and transcribed it in English. For instance, the word 'witches' in the title is not used in the book. I retained the word *yakshi* and chose not to use 'witches' in the text. Yakshi, for a person from Kerala, is a woman who is bewitchingly beautiful and alluring, who taps into man's eternal fascination or fixation on the perfect female form, and then traps him to a shocking, reprehensible tryst with death. She lives on top of toddy palm trees and waits for her prey beneath the frangipani tree. The only clue that gives her away is that, when she walks, her feet will not touch the ground! How can the English word – 'witch' – overlaid with very different mythical and cultural associations signify this South Indian variant? Here, in the south of India, there are instances where the sacred and the profane commingle in the loom of myth; where binaries like *eros* and *thanatos* vanish. The yakshi is a devourer, but she is also a temptress who spares the innocent, and a goddess who is worshipped in many a wayside shrine. When I had to translate the word *Pootham,* I retained that word along with its meaning in English (demon). I did that in some cases where the English word did not substantially alter the meaning of the original.

The text also has a liberal sprinkling of words in Tamizh and in the regional dialect of Nagercoil. I cross-checked the meaning of unfamiliar words, sometimes with the author himself, but more often with the poet–critic, Atmaraman (Bhaskaramenon Krishnakumar). I will count this endeavour as worthwhile if I have been able to share a fraction of the exhilaration and aesthetic satisfaction I felt while reading Jeyamohan's memoir.

1

Even Though

I

Taste of Medicine

Even though my mother had a lilting voice, she never sang; she recited poetry instead. For the average Malayalee, a good poem is an auditory experience. Ezhuthachan's[1] poetry is tender coconut water, Asan's[2] is honey and Changampuzha's[3] intoxicating wine. My mother discovered poetry in the heady days of her youth. She was barely eighteen when Changampuzha's *Ramanan* captured the imagination of the people of her village. She heard it for the first time while bathing in the temple pond. Her neighbour Thankamma had sung a couple of lines and she was hooked. She begged Thankamma to recite it once again, and then again. Those days, well-born women, especially pretty young girls like my mother, did not recite poetry. Poetry was the forte of the courtesan.

At Marthandam market at Karungal, you could get twenty sardines for twenty-five paise in those days. If you could scrimp for just four days and bought a few sardines less, you could buy a copy of *Ramanan*. My mother could not manage that. So she pinched a few coconuts from her house and sent them with her maid, Kali, to sell in the market and buy a copy of *Ramanan*.

Kali was the same age as my mother – with the same passions, the same dreams. They spent all their days together, inseparable. Kali did not know how to read or write, and mother … that was the only thing she knew. They sneaked into the woodshed, made themselves comfortable on the stacked coconut fronds, and read *Ramanan* and cried. They took the book with them to the temple tank, sat on the stone steps, read it, and cried again. They read it again and again and cried each time. Their age was such. There were only blossoms in their garden patch, no thorns or worms!

Much later, when I read *Ramanan*, I was quite taken aback. In Kerala, where do you find meadows where goats are taken out to graze? Over here, the usual practice is to rear cows in a barn. Maybe those cows dreamt of green meadows and a handsome shepherd boy with the Lord's own flute tucked at his waist – the boy who threw away that flute and killed himself for a girl.[4] He did not realize that he had a thousand *gopis* yearning for him.

Those days, if Mother or Kali hummed a line from *Ramanan*, the other would take it up and sing the rest. Sometimes they sang together. The only other song that drew so many tears was '*Manasa maine varu*'[5] from the lips of a Muslim youth who Takazhi and Ramu Karyat had transformed *Ramanan* into.

Mother moved away from Ramanan to Asan, from lost loves to unattainable loves. By then she was married to a domineering government servant and had become the mother of three children. She sighed with anguish at the pain of the fallen flower – *veena puvu* – for whom the sky was an elusive dream. She had moved away from the heady, youthful romance of earlier to the torment of the fallen woman. In the cold of early mornings, snuggled in my blanket, I would listen as she moved in the kitchen singing, 'Oh flower …!'

As she grew older, she discovered other, later poets, G. Sankara Kurup[6] and Poonthanam.[7] She was also fond of Vyloppilli.[8] But on no account would she accept Vallathol as a poet.[9] She was convinced that it was a conspiracy by the northern Malayalees to foist him on us as a poet. By the time she greyed, she became convinced that there was no poet to equal Ezhuthachan.

While I was growing up, my mother used to read the Ramayanam during the month of Aadi. Ten to twenty women would congregate in the evening to hear her. They took turns to bring the rice, coconut and jaggery needed for the offering. They came freshly bathed, their foreheads marked with sandalwood paste and holy ash. When my mother entered the hall carrying the lighted lamp, her wet hair adorned with a single flower, the women would rise up to greet the young scholar. She would reverentially place the lamp on the floor, arrange the pooja materials around it and sit down on the silk mat to read the *Adhyatma Ramayanam*.

There was an undertone of bell metal in my mother's voice. Her enunciation was good. One could float on her words, as if in a boat on a placid river. Some lines she read twice, sometimes thrice and, on rare occasions, she would pause and explain them. She infused the dramatic bits with proper emotion. The women hung on to her every word. They could never tire of listening to the story of Sita.

Once, while she was reading, I suddenly discovered that it was another poem! She was reading *Chintavishtayaya Sita* – the burning words of a woman against the cold-hearted impartiality of royal duty or *Rajadharma*. Her audience kept listening to her with bated breath, wide-eyed.

When she finished, one of the elder Brahmin ladies asked, 'Which is this song, Vishalam?'

My mother humbly replied, 'This is also *Ramayanam.*'

'Who is it by?' the lady asked sharply.

My mother lowered her head and whispered, 'Kumaran Asan.'

I thought the woman would cause a furore. Instead, she said softly, 'Read it once again.'

My mother had just given birth to my younger sister when she heard about Kali's suicide. Those days, polygamy was widely prevalent among the Pulayas.[10] If you had money, you could buy a Pulaya girl. Kali's husband had sold a cow in the market and bought a seventeen-year-old girl with that money. The moment that girl entered her house through the front door, Kali ran out of the back door and threw herself into the well. Her head hit a rock on the retaining wall and she was dead before her body hit the water.

After that incident, my mother did not enjoy Changampuzha's poems any more, especially *Ramanan.* It's a cursed poem, she lamented. By then she had discovered English writers and had started reading Thackeray, George Eliot, W.B. Yeats and, later, Hemingway. '*For Whom the Bell Tolls* is a modern classic,' she proclaimed. 'Restraint is an essential quality for a good writer, and there is no one who can lay claim to it as much as Hemingway.'

She definitely did not like Jayakanthan. 'You can read Janakiraman, but he is at bottom a romantic.[11] Infusing what is romantic into the emotional is forgivable. But doing it in matters related to vision and perception is not. 'You are too young to appreciate the difference now. You will understand it when you grow older.'

My mother suffered from acute insomnia. She was lucky if she could sleep for three hours. By the time she was forty-five she had become an old woman with grey hair. In our house, we did not have electricity. Whenever I woke up in the middle of the night, I would see her propped up on the bed reading books in the dim light of the kerosene lamp. That image is stamped in my mind's eye, like an old Venetian painting. When she was reading, there would be no expression on her face. The reddish light from the lamp reflected on her hair, and her eyes had the faraway look of a Rembrandt painting. Mother was extraordinarily beautiful. Even when she lost weight and her face had lost its lustre, her eyes glowed with the beauty of hidden dreams.

My mother loved *Les Misérables*. 'A model epic!' she used to assert. True, it is here that we encounter the sheer acme of perfection of the visionary romanticism,

I averred. She did not like M.T.[12] or Sarat Chandra or Bimal Mitra or S.L. Bhyrappa. Mere romantics, she would say, dismissing them, and seeking refuge again and again in *Les Misérables.* When I teased her about it, she said, 'Leave it, how can one live without at least a sliver of goodness?'

In 1985, in her fifty-fourth year, my mother committed suicide. Older people rarely take their own lives. For, with realization that you do not have many years left to live comes a renewed appreciation for life. Younger people take their own lives because of frustrations and disillusionments. But when it happens in old age, it could be because of some unknown metaphysical need.

One can identify many reasons for the manner of her death. One can say that all her life, in the fifty-four years of her existence, she had been moving towards that point. One can even say that she was collecting reasons and justifications for this act through her experiences. But sometimes I cannot but wonder if *Ramanan* has played a significant part in her decision to take her own life.

II

The Divine Demon[13]

Mother loved *Poothapattu*, 'The Song of the Divine Demon'. When she sang those lines, she turned into a Pulluva girl. I have always felt that among all the Malayalam poems, this is the one best suited for the lilting tune of a Pulluva song. Later, I have listened to many a rendition of the same song in impressive tones and tunes. But I consider my mother's rendition, in her soft, slightly dragging voice, the best. That poem captures the spirit of a village, and it is best sung in such a voice.

A slightly modified version of the story in *Poothapattu* exists in our village too. Once a demon from the hills came to see the village. He spies a small boy playing alone in the temple grounds and, captivated by his innocent looks, takes the boy back to his hilly abode. The distraught mother goes inside the shrine and vows to rip out her tongue and give up her life if she doesn't get her son back. The deity goes after the demon with his spear, defeats him in a fierce battle and brings back the child. Before chasing him back to his hilly abode in the forest, the deity gives the demon a boon. The demon could come to the village once a year during the temple festival of Mootharammankoda to see and kiss the boy. For a thousand years, the demon keeps visiting the village on the day of Mootharammankoda to see the boy. Living far away in the forest, the demon never realizes that the boy grew up to be a man, grew old and died. Instead, he searches for the young boy in every boy he sees!

In my mother's house at Nattalam there is a small mirror embedded in the wall. The plaster has been gouged out and the mirror fixed on the wall. Once when I visited her childhood home, my aunt pointed to the mirror and said, 'That's Vishalam's mirror. Even now, when you look at it you can see her face.' When she was young, my mother was very forgetful. She was always searching for misplaced things and, being pretty, she liked to see her face in the mirror all the time. So she had gouged out the plaster herself and fixed a small mirror in the hall.

It was a newly built house. When my mother's elder brother saw the desecration of the wall, he was furious. He was older than her by twenty years and was for all practical reasons the head of the family. Moreover, he was a prominent man in the village and was much respected. As soon as he saw the wall, he roared, 'Who did this?'

'I did it,' was my mother's nonchalant reply.

He rushed towards her with raised hands, but he couldn't hit her. She had his dead mother's face.

Averting his gaze, he said tightly, 'Leave.'

After this incident, my mother refused to look in the mirror. Initially, no one noticed it. My aunt, my mother's eldest sister, found out after three or four days.

'Brother did not say anything to you, then why can't you use it?' she inquired.

My mother did not respond. The other women in the house pleaded with her, her maids begged her to forget the incident and even the old granny next door told her to ignore her brother's anger. But to no avail.

Then the younger brother, who was also elder to her, drew her towards him and pleaded, 'It's okay, it is our elder brother, after all.' Mother wouldn't budge.

Two months passed before the eldest brother heard about it. He called her to his side. 'Leave it, dear, I scolded you in a moment of anger. Look at your face in the mirror. It's your brother who is telling you this.' Mother relented only then.

Mother married late. Both her elder sisters were married into families with a lot of landed property. Those times, most of the lands owned by Nairs were tied up in litigation. My uncle decided that the youngest sister should be married off to a man with a government job.

For Nair men, a government job in those days meant a job with the police or the army. My mother did not like either. Then came the proposal from my father. When he was very young, he had been injured and blinded in one eye. He was also partly bald. He had quarrelled with his own mother and was living alone. But he had a government job, did not drink and spoke politely. He had a reputation for being hot-headed and quick-tempered. My maternal grandfather was also known for his hot-headedness. According to village myth, he once beat a buffalo to death for attempting to gore him, and cried for a year over its loss. But all objections were brushed aside by Thankamakkan who brought the proposal. 'Look at her. She is so extraordinarily beautiful. He will curl at her feet like a tame kitten.' They got married in December 1960 at Kumaran Kovil.

My elder brother was born the next year, and a year after that, I was born. Our sister was born a year and a half later. All these years my mother was the victim of her husband's rages. Once, while she was carrying my sister, my father had grabbed the head of a palm frond and run towards the temple pond where mother was bathing and beat her up in front of everyone there for staying at the pond longer than he expected. Furious, my mother packed a bag and, taking her two children with her, went back to Nattalam. Soon after, Father received a legal notice with her signature. It was an *ozhimuri* – a divorce notice. Father came rushing to her house, stomping like a bull elephant and screamed obscenities at her entire family.

Her eldest brother, who also had a temper, rushed to the frontyard and slapped him across his face. Enraged, Father picked up a huge stone to attack Uncle and Uncle, in self-defence, picked up an iron bar that was lying around and hit him on the head. Father was in the hospital for seven months and he suffered its consequence for the rest of his life. As long as he lived, Father's hands shook due to the damage caused to his brain that day. During this entire period, Mother stayed at the hospital and looked after her husband, ignoring the wishes of her own family. But his own mother refused to visit him even once. 'Inform me when that scoundrel dies,' she scoffed.

Mother looked after her bedridden husband and her two infants all on her own. She had to give him the bedpan, clean him and feed him. And in return, all he did was abuse her and, when he could manage it, kick her. When she bent forward to feed him, he would spit on her. As soon as he could stand up from his bed, Mother arranged for a distant relative to look after him and left. He hadn't expected that. When she left, he sat without a word, without taking a morsel of food or a drop of water for two full days. He sat staring into space, his mouth clamped over a wad of betel leaves. Soon after this incident, he received the final divorce notice.

Meanwhile, Mother returned to her maternal home, close to term, holding the hands of her two young infants. As soon as he saw her, Uncle jumped out into the yard from the veranda and screamed, 'Why are you here? What business do you have here?'

Mother answered in a firm voice, 'Isn't this the house of Kaalivilakathu Padmavathi?

Uncle stared at her, his mouth hanging open in shock.

'I am her daughter, if someone does not like this fact then they can leave.' Saying this, she walked inside with firm steps, went to her room and changed her clothes.

That evening, in the temple courtyard, where the men usually gathered in the evening, Uncle declared, 'She is a witch, a yakshi, isn't she?'

Father sent many emissaries to plead with her. Through them he made multiple promises. Mother did not relent. Father longed to see the face of his newborn daughter. He started haunting the ochre-coloured lane in front of the Nattalam house. Mother pretended as if she did not even recognize the man. At one point, even her brothers pleaded with her to return to him.

'It is easy enough to divorce a man. But what will you do for the rest of your life? Even if you want to get married again, what will happen to your kids?' Mother was unmoved.

Father came to Nattalam for Shivrathri. He was desperate to talk to Mother. Her friends helped him covertly, and they saw each other face to face in front of the temple. She was carrying her three-month-old baby girl in her arms. He reached out to take the baby, his eyes full of unshed tears. She stepped back. 'Please move away,' she said, hurrying away from him. He stood there forlorn, and cried, heartbroken.

At the temple, someone gave me kheer with jaggery in it. It had verdigris and I ended up with diarrhoea. After two or three days, I was taken to a doctor in Kallugil. When I took the medicine I was given, the diarrhoea stopped. But it started again the moment I ate anything. Soon I was passing blood. They showed me to different doctors. By that time, twenty days had passed and I had become as emaciated as a rag doll. I couldn't retain anything except tender coconut water. I couldn't even move my arms or legs. Soon, I couldn't lift my head. I was admitted to the Mission Hospital at Marthandam.

While I was there, I showed signs of improvement, but relapsed the moment I got home. The doctors told my uncle that there was no point in hoping for a recovery.

When the diarrhoea stopped for eight days, my mother gave me a spoonful of rice gruel. Immediately it started again. I was passing blood and my body was racked by continuous shivering. My mother swaddled me in a white dhoti and rushed me to the hospital. As she was getting down from the bus, she saw Father. She was too distraught to even recognize her husband. He stood stunned by the sight of the bundle inside which I lay shrivelled like a dried fish. He ran forward, grabbed me from my mother's arms and ran through the crowded Marthandam market crying, '*Ayooo Ayooo.*'

Inside the bundle, I lay almost lifeless, soaked in pus, blood and faeces. They stained his white shirt and dhoti. My mother ran after us. Father took me straight to Dr Fletcher at Kulitoora Fletcher Hospital. There are two doctors who have entered the annals of the history of southern Travancore. They are Dr Fletcher and Dr Somerville – two doctor-missionaries who dedicated their lives to the service of the people. Dr Fletcher saved my life. He discovered that my problem was due to an allergy. While the other doctors had stopped giving me food, he fed me continually, in small quantities. My father stood there, day and night, feeding me gruel and water in tiny sips. He left my bedside to clean himself only on the third day. Slowly, my stomach settled down and within a week, I was eating solid food.

My father and mother patched up in the hospital. They quarrelled in the hospital and patched up again. From the hospital, Father took me to his place and Mother went with him. That is when she decided to let go of her family and her native place forever. She never went back. For twenty-two years she suffered his 'madness' and stayed with him. But as soon as her children had settled down in life, she took her own life.

While narrating these incidents to me fifteen years later, my mother told me, 'A mother will have a natural love for her kids. But isn't the love of the Demon who came searching for the boy for a thousand years, stronger than her love? That is why I decided to give my children to the Demon.'

III

The Hand

I was in the fourth standard when one morning I realized that I could not lift one of my hands. When I tried to force it up, the pain was so intense it was as though something was breaking inside. My skin was burning, my throat was parched and my dry lips stuck together. Those days we were living in Muzhukotti. The government hospital was four kilometres away at Arumana. Most of the time, the people of the village, reluctant to walk that far, would approach the Christian pastor for medicine. The pastor, Yeshuvadiyan, gave me a medicine for my fever. After three days, when the fever did not subside, they propped me up in the back of a cycle and took me to Arumana. The doctor wasn't there. As usual, the nurse prescribed some medicine and sent me home.

Father was away at a camp in Aral Vaymozhi and heard about my illness only when he returned. Though he was not someone who knew anything about children's illnesses, he felt a vague unease. He called a taxi and took me to the hospital at Marthandam. By then my right hand had swelled to the size of my thigh. The doctor at the hospital examined me for a long time. Then he called Father aside and told him, 'This is childhood rheumatism. It is too far advanced. Nothing can be done.'

My father folded his hands and tearfully pleaded, 'Please do something, Doctor. It's his right hand.'

'There is no hope. I have never seen a patient recover from this illness. His fever will go but we cannot save his arm.' The doctor was helpless.

Father brought me back home.

'What happened?' asked my mother anxiously.

'You whore! I will kill you and kill myself,' he shouted at her.

Mother carried me inside and lay me on the bed. I kept groaning in pain. Mother hugged me and cried for a long time. She must have drifted off to sleep. I could feel her soft breath on my skin like a benediction.

Outside on the veranda, Father sat sleepless on the easy chair. He sat there the entire night. I could hear him spit out betel juice or clear his throat. Sometimes he sighed heavily. I could occasionally hear the creak of the easy chair when he moved his weight. That night, both of us stayed awake. My arm lay beside me, a thing apart, an angry child demanding attention. It was filled with warm blood. It felt as though it wanted to tell me something. Intense pain does that to you. It severs you from yourself. It feels as though we are only the body, and at other times it feels as if we are anything but the body. The heartbeat and the pulse – the vacillation between these two. That whole night I throbbed like a clock keeping time. When morning came, Father had disappeared. Mother searched for him inside and outside the house. She sent people to the temple and the market looking for him. The betel nut seller consoled her. He had seen Father walking away from the house, early in the morning. He was wearing a fresh shirt and had his umbrella with him.

He must have walked far. It was noon by the time he returned. He came directly to the room where I was lying down. 'Does he have fever?' he asked.

Mother touched my forehead and said, 'Yes.'

When I saw my father, I started crying.

'Shut up, you bastard,' he shouted. 'You alone catch all the diseases in this world.' He raised his umbrella to hit me.

I screamed. Mother grabbed his arm. He shook her off and stormed out.

He sat on the easy chair again without a word. After some time, Mother went to him and asked quietly, 'Can I get you some water?'

'Whore!' he screamed, jumping up to hit her. 'I will mince you and throw you as fertilizer for the plantains.'

Mother ran inside and locked the bedroom door. He started kicking the door, shouting obscenities. He gave up suddenly and sat down heavily on the floor, leaning against the door. His eyes locked on the picture of Shastavu, Lord Ayyappa, and he turned his ire towards him. 'Scoundrel! Look at him sit. Why blame him? You should kick the man who worships him as God! Ungrateful wretch!'

In the afternoon, a *vaidyar*, an Ayurvedic doctor, arrived on a new cycle. His name was Anbayan. He had cycled fourteen kilometres to visit us. He did not wear a shirt. He wore a dhoti with a thin border of gold brocade. A smaller dhoti covered his head. A long gold chain adorned his hairy chest, and in his ears he wore emerald studs. Father hurried towards him.

He came inside, asking jovially, 'Now, young man, what trouble have you gotten into?'

As soon as he came near, I started crying loudly.

'Shame on you,' said the vaidyar. 'You, who belong to a clan of chieftains and should go fighting with a sword! How can you cry like this? No wonder that the British could kill Veluthambi. If his chieftains are like this, what hope does he have?' He sat down and twisted my arm. My cries died in my throat. My eyes started from their sockets and my whole body convulsed in pain. Mother screamed and Father turned around and slapped her hard. She ran away crying.

When the vaidyar stepped out of the room, Father asked, 'Is there any hope?'

The vaidyar said, 'Yes, it is childhood rheumatism. Poor boy. The swelling in his arm has become firm. I can't say anything for sure now.' He sat down in the veranda and drank a glass of buttermilk. As they shared a paan,

Father said, 'I do not have anyone to help me. You are my God.'

The vaidyar replied, 'I don't have any godly cures. My medicines will have to be taken exactly as prescribed. I will give you the medicine. But you have to strictly follow the dietary restrictions. Otherwise, the medicines won't work.'

'I will look after him with everything I've got,' my father said. 'He is a boy.'

The vaidyar patted him on the shoulder and said, 'I have looked at the boy's horoscope. He will become famous.'

The medicines started. In the morning there was a *leyham*. In the afternoon and evening there were *kashayams* – concoctions – to take. The dietary restrictions were severe. I couldn't take tea or coffee, sugar, salt, milk or buttermilk. No fruits, no vegetables. I could eat rice with a handful of drumstick leaves fried in coconut oil. I could not drink even a drop of water!

The May sun blazed overhead. Even the earth smoked. Unable to bear the heat, the trees folded their branches. They made a place for me to sleep beside the well so that it was cool. I bore my raging thirst listening to the sound of the water gently lapping inside the well. To prevent sweating and further loss of moisture, they wrapped me up in cool linen dipped in water.

When my mother brought the rice and drumstick leaves cooked without salt, the very smell was enough to make me throw up. Mother made balls of rice and greens and pleaded with me to eat them, 'Eat, sweetheart.' If Father was in the veranda and heard her, he would scream at me, 'I will come and beat you up to a pulp. Son of a dog. Eat now. You get diseases that people haven't even heard of and then play the innocent. Mangy dog.' Mother would lower her voice and plead tearfully, 'Eat a little bit.'

On the first day of the treatment itself, Father had issued an ultimatum. 'If I hear that you have drunk even a drop of water, you son of a dog, I will kill you.' He called my brother and younger sister and warned them, too. He warned Eziliyamma, our domestic servant, and even the neighbour, Vijayan. Anyway, they were too shocked by my appearance to come near me. I suffered greatly and would cry for just a drop of water. My mother, teary-eyed, would implore, 'Please don't cry. Your throat will get parched.'

After a week the massage with medicated oil started. Anbayan vaidyar would arrive early morning on his cycle. As soon as I heard the sound of the cycle I would start screaming. He would sit on the cot next to me and tease me, 'Nair boys should not cry.' Then he would take each of my fingers and bend it. Each time he did that, my whole body shook with unbearable pain and I would scream, beating my legs on the cot. Unable to bear my screams, Mother would flee to the neighbour's house. As he worked his way up my arm, my throat would become parched from screaming so much and no sound would come out.

The vaidyar was unmoved. 'You should teach him music,' he quipped, cleaning the oil off his palms. 'He will sing beautifully.'

Father would be sitting in the veranda in his easy chair. 'The boy should have an oil massage every day,' the vaidyar told my father. 'But above all, what is important is the medicine.' A tender coconut would be kept aside for the vaidyar. He would drink it and cycle back.

After his morning ablutions and breakfast, Father would come to my bedside for the second round of oil massage at around 10 a.m. As soon as I saw him, I would clamp my mouth shut with my left hand and scream soundlessly. By the time he finished the massage I would be left only half-conscious with pain. In the afternoon, he would walk six kilometres home in the blazing sun for the third massage. Then in the evening, another massage and once more at night, around nine o'clock, before going to bed. If I made any sound, he would beat me.

Sleep for me was the ebbing of terrible pain. I slept the whole day. At night I stayed awake. Always, I sensed Father outside the room. When I called out to Mother softly at night, Father would come to the door.

'What?' he would ask brusquely.

'I want to pee,' I would murmur.

He would not lift me up tenderly like my mother would. It was more like an eagle snatching up a chicken. He would take me to the base of the coconut tree and, after I was done, carry me back to the cot without a word.

After fifteen days of this routine, I was allowed to sip warm water. When I heard that, I cried with joy. Even the very word 'water' sounded sweet to my ears. The vaidyar said, 'Earlier, when people took medicine for fifteen days without water, the practice was to drink urine for three days. Will the child drink urine? If you drink urine for ten days, the body will never crave for tea or coffee.' However, when I drank water I threw up. The next time I saw water, I felt nauseous.

My exercises also started on the fifteenth day. It was the beginning of an experience that reduced all the suffering I had endured till then to nothing. Every day Father would take me to the front of the house where there was a grille portion. I had to lift my right hand

and keep it on the lower rung of the grille. Even the thought of lifting the arm was painful, and though the heart desired it the arm refused to move. 'Keep your hand on the grille,' roared Father, raising his cane. I couldn't. The cane would come down with force on my buttocks. When the cane landed a second time, I would scream and grab the bar. Then I had to lift my hand to the next rung. Again, the cane would land. For some reason, I could move the dead weight of my arm only with the momentum gained through extreme fear and pain. I had to lift my arm up six rungs and bring it down the same way.

The first day, when mother heard my screams, she came running out of the house and grabbed the cane. Maddened, my father began hitting her. She fell to the ground, covering her face with her hands. In the melee, Father did not even notice that he had lost his dhoti. He stood there in his striped boxer shorts shouting, 'Lift, you bugger! Lift your arm.'

On the fourth day, unable to bear my cries, our neighbour Narayanan rushed over to our house. 'Bahuleya, don't murder that kid. The curse of the very young can blight your life.' Father lifted up his cane and stepped forward, threatening the eighty-five-year-old man. 'I will kill all of you bastards.'

A month of this and the pain abated a bit. I could lift my arm on my own. First ten times, then twenty, then a hundred. Later for an hour. Father would sit in a chair with the cane in his hand and count. Within sixty days, my hand had returned to normal. For a year after that, there was a slight weakness in that arm. There were no long-term ill effects. I have written thousands of pages using that arm, sixty books to be exact.

It was a miracle. Those days, childhood rheumatism was quite prevalent. Many homes had at least one person who had suffered its ill effects. Many doctors came to visit me to see my recovery for themselves. When people came, Father would call me and ask me to lift my arm. Later, when people came, I would take off my shirt myself and get ready to lift my arm in front of them. I was taken to Trivandrum to show people the full recovery of my arm. That was when I had the opportunity to see the clock tower, the Methanmani, and the east fort, Kizhakekotta.

One day, while returning from school, I saw vaidyar Anbayan standing in a paan shop. With him was an old man. The vaidyar beckoned me over. The old man examined my right arm. He pulled and squeezed it. 'This is amazing,' he said, 'the arm has recovered fully. I have never seen muscles recover this well.' The vaidyar smiled, 'These days, who trusts our medicine for their children? What helped him was his father's insistence. The boy will survive, the father might not.' He placed his hand on my head and said, 'He is a good boy, blessed by Sarasvati.'

Father could never believe that I had recovered fully. Even when I was a full-grown man, the moment he saw me his eyes would anxiously drift towards my arm. Later, whenever I fell ill with a fever or something and when Mother went up to him to inform him of it, his anxiety would resurface.

Mother would say, 'The boy has fever.'

'Hmm.'

He would not say anything more. Would not come to check on me. But when the whole house had slept, he would come, on silent feet, and stand next to the bed. I would hear his deep sigh. Then he would bend and press my right arm and shoulder. I wouldn't be sleeping. Yet I would not open my eyes. If I did, I would lose something that I admired and cherished.

Father did not pay Anbayan vaidyar any money. The vaidyar was an extremely rich man for whom treatment was service. Nevertheless, for fifteen years the vaidyar would send his destitute patients to our house. They would come with torn clothes and weary faces.

Father would invite them in and give them food and money. He would call me to his side and ask me to pay obeisance to them, and he would ask them to bless me.

Once, much later, I was talking to my mother about Father. Among all the men I have met in my life, I have never seen someone who was as fond of fish as Father. He was so fond of fish that when his daughter got married, he did not partake of the feast because there was no fish. In fact, I can confidently say that he never ate without fish. His favourite deity was the Matsyavatara of Lord Vishnu. But if the *avatara* was not careful he would cut him up and make a curry out of him! He never skimped on buying fish either. While returning from the office, he generally had a packet of fresh fish in hand.

'If your name had been Meenakshi, instead of Vishalakshi, he wouldn't lose his temper so much with you,' I once teased Mother.

She suddenly became serious.

'You should never say that. When you ate rice and drumstick leaves for sixty days, he did not touch a morsel of fish. Do you know that? The first day of your treatment, after Anbayan Vaidyar left, he sat down to eat lunch. There was fried mackerel and a curry made of king mackerel. He came and sat down on the floor to eat and stared at the food. His head shook. The next moment, he kicked away the plate and bellowed, "Take this away, you daughter of a scoundrel. Her mother's fish curry."

'After that, for sixty days, he ate the same drumstick leaves and rice that you ate. I also tried it for two or three days, but I gave up and made rice and curry for myself. He would come and sit in front of the food. As soon as he saw the food, he would lose his temper and stalk off. It is sheer good fortune that you recovered. Otherwise, he would have killed a few people on the road and killed himself. He is a raging savage, no?'

IV

Memorial

In my father's life, the house in Muzhukotti proved to be a turning point. We had never lived in such a spacious house. The constant transfers and the rented accommodations they entailed meant that we had to make do with what was available. Often, we had to settle for granaries. Caught in litigation, the Aniyattu house in Muzhukotti lay vacant for many years. Father rented it for twenty rupees a month. Located in the centre of a two-acre plot, the house was massive. It was at least a hundred years old and had a gatehouse, a guest house and a woodshed attached to it. The gatehouse was itself rather large. We children put up a swing there and enjoyed ourselves. The compound was full of coconut and jackfruit trees and thickets. It looked like a small forest with narrow footpaths snaking through it. The house had the grandeur of a Nair homestead. This house aroused the aristocratic impulses lying dormant in my father.

My father belonged to an aristocratic family. He had lost his father when he was an infant. After her husband's death, his mother, Lakshmikutti, sold parcels and parcels of land she owned to fund her various court cases. Later, she married another man, had children by him, divorced him, married again and then again. By the time my father reached the eighth standard, he had broken off all ties with his mother. He completed his school education with money borrowed from well-wishers. After his eleventh class, he left home and started living on his own.

After that he had never had a house to call his own. Throughout this period, he supported himself by giving tuitions to younger children. He stayed at the house of his pupils and ate what was given to him. His first job was in a ration shop. Later, he got a government job in the Tamil Nadu registration office. For most of his life, Father worked in areas where Tamizh was spoken. Later, he begged for a transfer to Malayalam-speaking areas and got a posting in his native place. During the remaining thirty years of his service, he only went to proper Tamil Nadu twice, and each time, for just a day. He would go to Trivandrum once a year, for the temple festival. The rest of the time he spent in South Travancore.

This does not mean that he led a sedate life. He was always up and about. Kathakali, temple festivals, elephants, checking out cattle, visiting temples, court cases – all these things kept him busy. He had a soft spot for his dead father's native place – Thiruvarambu. He had lived there for only four years as an infant, but he decided that it was his native place, too. Wherever he was, he got involved in the affairs of Thiruvarambu and was on the organizing committee of the temple festival there. His father's ancestral house lay in ruins to the south of the temple. According to native custom, it had passed through the female line, and now lay abandoned. When he visited the temple, he would visit the empty house and sit silently on the broken stone steps.

Father started creating a homestead at the Muzhukotti house. It already had a sturdy cowshed. Father bought four cows and installed them in the shed. He put a chair in the shed and stayed up all night picking out blood-sucking fleas from the cows. Then he bought a dog. The dog became his trusted servant and stayed under his easy chair whenever he was at home. Then he bought a long ladder with twenty-one rungs and tied it up in the veranda. Those days we had neither land nor coconut plantations which would justify buying such a tall ladder.

'What madness is this?' asked his old barber, Pachi. Pachi was the only person who could chastize Father.

Father replied shortly, 'Let it be. It is auspicious.'

'Then buy some land or a coconut plantation,' retorted Pachi.

'I will,' said Father, 'But not here.'

'If you have a harvest there, why have a ladder here?' countered Pachi.

'I am not there. I'm here,' responded father.

'That's true!' said Pachi. He understood that logic well.

Father bought land and a paddy field in Thiruvarambu. He would go there by bus to oversee the farming. Because the law said that the same group that harvestes the crop had to thresh it too, he loaded the harvested paddy and the workers onto a cart and transported them the twenty kilometres to our house. People were so surprised to hear about this that they gathered in front of our house to see it for themselves!

'Wouldn't it be cheaper to thresh it there and bring just the paddy?' asked Eziliamma.

'Get lost, you bitch,' retorted Father, smiling. 'What do you know?'

Mother, who had sent her, stood hidden behind the door cursing him soundlessly. Eziliamma just said, 'Who will he listen to, Ammini? You don't say anything. Who can separate the gold from the dirt?'

A haystack on one side; next to it, a pit for cow dung; farm implements stacked in a corner of the veranda ... but Father was not satisfied. He went and bought a wooden plough. People started arriving at our doorstep to see this odd man.

'Sir, instead of cow dung, you should add *chavanprash* for a good crop of rice,' mocked Anthoni master from the lane.

'Get lost, you scoundrel,' said Father, smiling indulgently.

In the kitchen, Mother threw a vessel in frustration and said, 'When you become shameless, you need no clothes.' She took out her anger on my sister. 'Drop dead, you useless girl.'

My father was a man who spent his money carefully. I call him a 'careful spender' because he was my father. If he was someone else's father, I would have called him a miser. There was only one person in the entire village who would bargain over the price of even a cup of tea.

He was an expert in family law, especially the law on the Hindu undivided family. So, apart from his salary, he had a fairly good income. He kept buying land and soon owned extensive property in Thiruvarambu. At last, he got what his heart had yearned for. He was able to buy the land that had belonged to his father's family. Next to the land he bought stood his father's old family homestead – 'Ganapathy Vilakam' – crumbling, ready to fall. Its current owner refused to sell the house and the eight cents of land on which it stood.

Father took us to show us the land. He walked around almost in a daze, touching each coconut palm. Watching him, I quipped, 'Father looks like Armstrong walking on the moon.' That evening, lying in his armchair, he called Mother. His voice was sweet. There was half an hour of friendly conversation followed by fierce fighting – this was the usual ritual. Mother came from the kitchen wiping her wet hands.

'I am thinking of building a house. What do you say?' This meant that he had already started work on the house. He stood up, went to his box and, opening it, showed her some papers. They were accounts of projected expenditure. Obviously the result of months of labour.

As soon as he started talking about the house, Mother realized that he had a tiled house in mind. '*Ayyoo*, is it a tiled house? Let us build a terrace house. Who builds a house with roof tiles these days?'

Father's demeanour changed. 'Shut up, you bitch. Will anyone decent build a terrace house? Looks like a chicken coop. I hate the very sight of it. Any well-born Nair will stack wood and build a house. You won't understand. You have to be born into an aristocratic family to understand that.'

The moment Father started abusing her family, Mother would lose her temper. A verbal fight ensued, which rapidly became physical. In anger, Father caught hold of the almirah and upended it. The crashing sound alerted the neighbours – Pillai was on the rampage. That quarrel lasted the entire night.

People pleaded with Father not to build a tiled house. The price of the wood alone would be exorbitant. There were no skilled carpenters. Tiled houses were unsafe. Father did not budge. When he heard an opinion different from what he had decided, he would sit quietly, carefully trimming a wad of tobacco and would start chewing it.

He had already decided who his carpenter would be, ten years ago. Pundarikam Kumaran Ashari belonged to a family of illustrious carpenters. In the olden days, the family had built the Maharaja's palace. The Krishnan Kovil Palace had been built by his father.

Father, on his own, decided the place and date for beginning work on the house. Mother was still sulking.

The carpenter had to draw the *vastu mandala*, hammer in the stakes and tie the thread between the stakes to mark the lines of the foundation. To do that, Father brought in Kumaran Ashari's father, Paraman Moothashari. He was an old man, well over ninety. His eyesight and hearing were still good, but he had lost all his teeth and his jaw kept moving constantly, as though he was chewing something. His head, chest, arms and legs were covered in curly white hair and looked as if they were lathered in soap. His neck had knotted veins standing out prominently. As soon as he arrived in a bullock cart, he said he had to urinate. I took him under a huge tree. He removed his sacred thread and squatted. Urinating was obviously painful for him, and he kept calling out to the gods – 'Muruga, Velappa, Kumarappa!' When he stood up, he turned towards the temple and paid obeisance.

He asked, 'Where is the land?'

Father came forward and respectfully led him towards the designated place. The old man looked at Father in shock and said emphatically, 'A house will not last here, Nair.'

A red-hot spark glowed in Father's eyes. He just said tonelessly, 'This is the place.'

'This place does not have a proper left and right. A door in the east won't last here, and a door in the north is inauspicious. Don't do it,' the old man explained.

My father just said, 'This is the place where I am building the house.'

The old man looked at his son and asked in a harsh voice, 'What kind of calculations have you done, you mongrel wretch? What?' He raised his hand to slap his son.

His son moved away and said, 'That's why I begged you to come.'

'When did I not come with you, you bastard?' The old man was in a temper.

The son dragged his unwilling father back to the bullock cart. The old man was still trying to slap his son. Father turned to me in anger. 'What are you looking at? Get lost.'

Kumaran Ashari came back. Father said, 'Hurry, we are losing time. Everything goes as decided earlier.'

Mother and Eziliamma were standing a little distance away, under the shade of a large tree. Mother sent me to call the carpenter. When he came reluctantly towards her, Mother asked, 'What is the problem, Kumara?'

'Nothing Ammini, nothing,' he said in an unsure voice.

'What did Moothassari – the elder carpenter – say?' Mother persisted.

'Oh! He has some old calculations in his mind. Those calculations are all wrong. He's old, no?'

'No. What he says is significant,' said Mother.

'He wants a door facing the east as well,' Kumaran Ashari said, averting his eyes.

'What did he say exactly? Tell me the truth.' Mother's eyes sharpened.

'Something like that.' The carpenter started moving away.

'Ashari, swear on your daughter. What did he say exactly?'

The carpenter turned towards her in anger. 'What does that have to do with my daughter? I am a labourer. According to the shastras, only a building with a doorway to the east will last on this land. But there is not enough room here to build a house facing east. I have explained all of it to your husband. Ask him. Don't bring my children into it.'

Mother looked stunned. In shock, Eziliamma covered her mouth with her hand.

My mother's large, beautiful eyes swam in tears. 'Ashari, is this true?'

The carpenter tried to mollify her, 'Ammini, these are old calculations. Who pays any heed to all this these days? We can build a small door facing east, to pay lip service to the shastras.'

'Can we cheat the shastras, Ashari?'

'Ammini, please don't create any issues. How do they build houses in Nagercoil? On the street, who bothers about north and east? Over there, whatever the layout, people build houses. What is the problem with that?'

'That's different, Ashari,' said Mother. 'The shastra for a house on a street is different. When you build houses next to each other on a street, the *vastu* for the entire row is calculated as one.'

'Ammini, I have said what I had to say. You discuss the matter with your husband and decide.'

Mother folded her hands in prayer and pleaded, 'I have to live there with my kids.'

'Tell that to your husband,' retorted the carpenter.

She walked up to her husband. But before she could even utter a single word, he slapped her. Hard. She was saved because Ezili ran and caught her before she fell. While the groundbreaking ceremony was going on, Mother was lying tearfully on the veranda next to the temple. Father was in high spirits. Wearing a tilak of sandalwood paste, a turban and an upper cloth with a gold border, he moved around, happily supervising things.

'How many *kol*[14] is it?' asked Vazhakara Kumara Pillai.

'Twenty kol,' said Father, 'might increase.'

'One structure?'

'Yes.'

'Then the height will be around forty feet?' Kumara Pillai looked at Ganeshan Nair.

'Have you seen the old Ganapathy Vilakam house?' asked Father.

'No. By the time I came here, it was already in ruins,' replied Kumara Pillai.

'It was the tallest structure in Thiruvarambu. This will be taller than that by ten feet.'

'That's what you have in mind!' smiled Kumara Pillai.

'Of course. I named my house twenty years ago. My house will be known as "Ganapathy Vilakam Mekkeveedu". Do you like it?'

Food was arranged for everyone at the temple premises. Mother served the rice and payasam. Father could not sit still and kept returning to the site, next door. He examined the strings tied to the stakes and sat down on the stump of a coconut tree that had been cut to clear the ground. Emotions flitted across his face like the rippling reflections from a pond.

Father could never complete that house. Money drained away. He was never satisfied. After getting a job, I moved away to Kasaragod. Brother also got a job and shifted to Nagercoil. Our younger sister got married and settled down in Trivandrum. Father retired. He spent all the money he got upon retirement on the house. The bickering between Father and Mother increased.

One day, when Father returned from the fields, he saw that all the doors and windows of the house were locked from the inside. He knocked, and when he didn't get a response, he broke open a windowpane. Mother had hung herself from one of the beams.

After that my father lived only for another fifty-six days. On hearing the news about Mother, I came down from Kasaragod. On the third day, I left without speaking a word to Father. My brother left as he had no leave from work as he was still on probation. My sister's mother-in-law was ailing, so she left soon, too. Father ended up alone in that huge house. He shuttered all the rooms and took to spending time in the veranda. He ate his food, ordered from a hotel nearby. During the night, he would light a lamp and spend his time in the veranda without sleep. His only companion was his dog.

Fifty-five days after mother's death, he locked up the house, threw away the key and left the village. He wanted to die in a land where no one would recognize him. He went to Cherthala beach and drank poison. The fishermen there saw him and took him to the government hospital. Someone recognized him there. He got better. He informed them that he had no intention of returning home and that he would prefer to stay somewhere in Trivandrum. But fate willed otherwise. The poison had reached the ulcer in his stomach. Through that it entered his bloodstream. He passed away the next day. After the post-mortem, the body was not taken home. It was taken to the Crematorium at Thekkevila and consigned to the flames.

All three of us had hated that house. It lay there abandoned for four years. Then we sold it. Since no one wanted to live in the house, the new owner, Appiperuvattan, demolished it and sold the timber. He levelled the land and planted rubber trees on it. I doubt whether any mark of that house has survived. In the past twenty-five years, neither my brother, my sister nor I have ever visited Thiruvarambu. Much later, my sister-in-law showed me an old ration card with the address of that house. When I asked my brother why he still kept it, he pointed to the name of the house with a bitter smile.

V

The Last Drunkard

It was a rainy night in 1985. In the neon light, the endlessly falling rain glowed golden. I reached the liquor shop. I hadn't slept in days. The isolation I lived in would intensify in the night. All illnesses intensify at night. Isolation is also a kind of disease. Sleep would seize me unawares like a wave – for a few minutes. I would wake up in a strange place. In the street, in the office. I would hear strange sounds. Mother calling me. Scenes from the past would pass in front of my eyes:

Mother's smile.
Mother walking on the narrow ridge between the fields.
The dog following her.
The yard in front of the house in the golden glow of the afternoon sun.
The sounds from the kitchen in the morning.

'Mother!' I would cry out, waking up with a start. I would be lying on the roadside, the sound of rushing traffic in my ears.

I stood outside the liquor shop, leaning against a lamp post. There was a weird taste in my mouth. I kept clearing my throat and spitting. People were walking into the shop constantly. Some walked in purposefully, tying up their dhotis. Others hurried in as though for an appointment. Some came alone, others in groups. The door to the liquor shop resembled an anthill. You could never say that the man who came out was the same man who went in.

The place I stood in had been a workshop, now long abandoned. Rusted old machine parts lurked, wet and dark, between overgrown thickets of *communist pacha* (Siam weed). Swarms of mosquitoes emerged from the undergrowth and surrounded me. I moved one bare leg over the other and kept wiping my face with my hands in a futile attempt to protect myself from their onslaught. I must have dozed off.

Once again, I was in front of our house.
The cows, the hayricks, the threshing yard, all looked exactly the same.
Inside the house, someone was singing.
A person laughed and another came to the veranda and emptied a glass of water in the yard.

A stray dog came over and stood humbly next to me. Its tail moved once, apologetically.

It is through great losses, tribulations and humiliations that we learn about the reality of our minds. We enter a dark space – without any doors – where we are confronted with an endless stream of inner monologues; or we feel we are locked up in a room with four of five mad people for company; or caged in an empty, silent room with white walls and a white floor and ceiling, for eternity. We start feeling detached from the body. This out-of-body experience itself is scary. If we reach out to catch it, it disappears like a whiff of smoke. Yet, if we ignore or try to forget its existence, it sits like heavy granite over our thoughts. If its tail breaks off and throbs in death throes, it turns to watch the tail impassively, unblinkingly.

I was running away from my mind, in fear of it. I was possessed by an ogre and I had no clue how to exorcize it. It was leading me into a bottomless pit. I could see the darkness towards which it was leading me, but I still surrendered, screaming silently. The monster was with me on the seashore, in the temple and by the riverside. A garrulous monster that talked incessantly and wept. Whenever I saw a madman, my insides would throb with anxiety. Was I mad? But if one asks that question of oneself, one could not be mad, no? But did that mad man also feel the same way? He was enthusiastically picking up all the papers from the ground. Maybe in search of a paper he had lost – sometime, somewhere, long ago.

I realized with clarity that sleep was the panacea for my illness. If only I could sleep with abandon, I'd be cured. My mind was a confused mess – like a library where the books had spilled from upended shelves and got mixed up. I convinced myself that everything would sort itself out – if I could only sleep. I tried to sleep again and again, in darkened rooms, blindfolded to keep the light out, stuffing my ears with scrunched-up cotton to cut out the noise. I would go to sleep when the desire to sleep would become overwhelming and I would slip effortlessly into a deep slumber. Ten minutes, maybe twenty would pass. I would wake up, my body shivering.

What did I find there?

A tunnel. In the dark, the flap of wings, sobbing. Who is it? In that dark, haunted place, where strange events jostled for space with stranger events, the doors creaked open, inviting you in. Inside, the Ogre sits. My senses screamed, 'There is a yakshi in there. She is the war goddess. She will decimate your entire clan. She sits there, eyes peeled, thirsting for blood. She sits, her scarlet mouth open, in front of the sacrificial altar that reeks of blood!'

I did many things to fall asleep. I would walk miles and miles till I was ready to collapse from sheer physical exhaustion. I would oil myself and bathe in cold water. I would eat old rice gruel. I realized that these things flowed away like cold water without quenching the burning lava inside me. That was when I sought the arrack shop.

Father never drank. He had tried alcohol while he was young and had decided that it was not meant for a gentleman. In his eyes, anyone who was not in control of his own actions was not a man. A drunkard was doomed to constantly apologize for his actions. A man's life, if he had to stoop to apologize, was not worth living. Even when he physically hurt someone, a good Nair should be able to take responsibility for it and say, 'Yes, I caused hurt.'

He lived by his tenets. Not because they were divine laws. He cared two hoots about divine laws or God or elders. He lived a righteous life because, in his opinion, an unrighteous man had to suffer humiliations everywhere and beg forgiveness from everyone.

Father came with me to my college admission. After we arrived at the college and paid the fees, Father turned to me and spoke for the first time.

'Come,' he said. He walked up to a nearby mango tree and we stood in its shade. Its trunk was covered with termites. He started brushing them off with his bare hands. I stood next to him, silent.

Father never spoke to me directly. He would talk to my elder brother – tell him about family matters and about what was happening on the farm. To my mother he only spoke what was strictly necessary. He would hold my sister close and show affection. In fact, he showed affection to all the little kids in the village.

Me! He wouldn't even look at me. When he wanted to tell me something, he would say it aloud to my brother or mother within range of my hearing. I had never even heard him mention my name. I knew that when he spoke about 'the boy', he meant me, just as when he mentioned 'Blackie', the dog knew it was his name. The only time Father spoke to me directly was that one time on 3 June 1979, at eleven o'clock in the morning.

Even now, he wasn't talking to me. He spoke to the wind.

He said, 'I know you. You are not like him. Listen. I have said what I have to. If you walk the straight path, good for you.'

He proceeded to tell me three things.

One: 'Never drink. It won't work for you. If you start drinking, you will end up on the road.'

Two: 'Be with one woman. Lust is not as great as it is made out to be. If you vacillate, women will make you mad.'

Three: 'You do not have a head for business. When you want to buy something or enter into transactions involving large amounts, always consult your brother. He will be there for you even when I am no longer there. I have spoken to him and he has agreed.'

The power of words that are never repeated is indeed infinite. I have never broken his injunctions. However, after I lost both Father and Mother, when I wandered around like a restless ghost, my legs took me to an arrack shop. I was looking for an escape. I longed to free myself from my stinking reality and forget myself for a few minutes. But I had never once had the courage to enter the shop. I would stand in front of that white board with its bold red letters – Arrack – for hours. There was a small lighted bulb above its door, bleeding yellow like pus. The iron door was wide open. Snippets of conversation splashed out now and then, like foam from a churning pail of buttermilk.

I was worried that someone would ask me something. I composed dozens of answers in reply to those imaginary questions. No one asked me anything. Apparently, it wasn't unusual for a young man to stand there on his own. I began to long for someone to ask me something.

'Son, what do you want?'

'What happened?'

'Where are you headed?'

The more they ignored me, the more agitated I got. I longed to curse and abuse them. I longed to throw stones at them. My insides filled with profanities. When I saw myself suddenly filled with expletives, I was shocked.

When my feet started hurting, I squatted there. The rain became heavy. A nearby tree dripped water from its leaves. Water dropped from swaying, wet coconut fronds, as though from newly washed hair. You could see the rain in the pools of light – like amber smoke, like a swarm of bees. The trees sighed in the cold wind that started blowing. A blue polythene cover became animated and started racing towards my feet, got caught in a bush and flapped its wings. A dog got up, shook his body to get rid of the water, stretched and disappeared behind me. I saw that he had made a warm lair in the dry sand beneath a rusting iron sheet. The wind blew again. Coconut palm fronds swirled. In the empty lot behind the arrack shop, a palm leaf fell heavily.

On the main road, further away, vehicles spilled light as they sped away. The wet leaves burned in the sudden flash of light that fell on them and were extinguished. Building walls sloughed off shadows that twisted and dropped down, only to escape into the darkened sky. The shadow of the lamp post caressed the arrack shop and lengthened towards the south. When there was a break in traffic, the road lay dark, pregnant with expectation.

My water-soaked clothes clung to my skin. I hadn't noticed the rain become heavy. My pocket was filled with water. I squeezed it dry, like a breast.

Why am I standing there? The thought flashed now and then. I will enter that door. I will get drunk and, like that polythene cover, I will blow with the wind.

The number of vehicles on the road decreased. It became quiet. The rain stopped. The wind picked up speed, scattering raindrops on the walls. I stood up. Pulled my shirt straight. Then sighed and leaned back on the lamp post once again. That night, I entered that door many times in my mind. A clock struck somewhere. Its ring went on and on, and then stopped.

The whole city was asleep. Not a soul stirred. Maybe they were all dead. From inside the arrack shop, someone helped a man to move out. The man kept mumbling, 'Let me finish buddy … let me say … say ...' He struggled. The man who ushered him out was a strong-looking guy in a faded T-shirt. He wore his dhoti tucked up to his knees. The protesting man was around forty, thin and dark. The other man pushed the iron grille door shut.

The man outside kept pleading, 'Buddy, stop, listen to what I have to say.' He clung to the grille. The man inside was least bothered. He locked up the shop. The yellow light went out.

'What manners is this?' the man wondered aloud.

'What? Let me finish … look here man …' He was talking to the door. As time passed, the door kept losing its door-ness and became more and more wall-like. The drunkard pointed at the door and muttered something. He stood there staring at it for some time and suddenly, without any warning, burst into tears. His sobs rent me into two. My legs shook. Unable to bear his pain, the man kept beating his breasts.

'I'll die. I'll die,' he screamed. His screams flooded the empty street like a terrible curse. I found my dry lips stuck together.

I longed to go to him, hug him close, comfort him and dry his tears. But there was no connection between my mind and body. The man stumbled towards me. He stopped in front of me and peered at my face. Our eyes met. I saw his teary eyes. I was weeping inside. He looked as though he wanted to say something but didn't.

He moved on … away from the circle of light of the lamp post. I, too, had to go his way. I walked in the opposite direction.

VI

Notes

It was in the eighties, while I was wandering restlessly, on the brink of madness, that I met Sundara Ramaswami. I started writing letters to him – two or three every day – some of them over a hundred pages long. I used to write copiously even before. Maybe it was this habit; Ramaswami said my language was good. Many of those lines were poetry. A select few reached Ramaswami's press. That's how I became a writer.

After those emotions – the impetus behind those poems – died, I stopped writing poetry. I realized that poetry was not my medium. I am a novelist.

One night, when I almost lost my mind, I wrote in a letter that I never sent.

I had never realized how long this night would be, nor the strangeness of time, which lengthens as we take count of it. Who thinks of others when they are alone? I have seen the beast that eats itself, the one with an insatiable hunger. Oh friend, friend, do you know what it is to lose again and again? Do you know that as time passes the weight of being increases exponentially for those who are condemned to live only in the past? Friend, do you realize what it is that we are losing incessantly? Unspoken words sprout. In the dampness of our blood, there are things with us that we do not know of.

Friend, now I think of them, the ones who are gone, they must exist in some other world. (Can one remember those who did not exist?) What have they taken with them? Leftovers? Residues? Salted memories? Where are they? What are they doing? I want to know now. I will stake my very existence on these questions. Have they discussed it at least now, why they hated each other so much? Have they understood the reason at last?

The House of Wind*

Into the abandoned house
the wind alone enters
naturally, solitary
moving the windowpanes
caressing the walls.
It flows through
the empty rooms,
blows on cobwebs
gathers the dust together
to leave it next to the walls.

---

*Written in 1987. Published in 1992.

Fingers the cast-off objects
one by one, smilingly.
before leaving
in the fragile pages of dust
leaves an unknown message.

Balichoru – Offering for the dead*

The flames rage
my clan is burnt.
On a green plantain leaf
aubergine and sesame
the strange-smelling balichoru.
Among those cawing with inclined heads
which one is you?
Father, assuage your hunger
this rice is for you.
When I turn away with the rice ball
the river stretches, a road of empty sand.
In my hands, the drying rice
I alone have no water
Ganga, Cauvery,
Kashi and Kanyakumari,

---

*Written in 1986 and published in 1988 in Sundara Ramaswamy's *Kalachuvadu – Footsteps of Time*. Can be considered my first published piece.

I wander,
carrying your balichoru,
like a holy Kavadi on my shoulder.
I just need water – knee-deep.
To submerge and cleanse.
In which ancient palm leaf
or rock engraving
can I find resolution?
You may not have hunger and thirst
I am the one who struggles
this is my balichoru.

VII

Hiranyan

It was my elder brother who told me that there was a Kathakali performance in Tripparappu Kovil – *Hiranyavadham*. Feisty performance. You will pay to watch just the last scene, he said. They had also made arrangements to travel there by boat. 'Are you coming?'

I did all my chores dutifully and then approached Mother for permission. 'Let Father come.' Her reply was short. I was on pins and needles.

As usual, Father came home late. Outside, it was getting dark. From the nearby temple, there arose a couple of calls – the signal to start our journey for the performance. Father came in, washed his hands and feet and sat down in his easy chair to enjoy his paan. All this while Mother and I were talking silently with our eyes. I pushed her to the veranda with my eyes.

She stood, partially hidden by the door, and said softly, 'Today there is Kathakali in Tripparappu.'

Father was silent.

She looked at me. 'The boy asks if he can go.'

Father cleared his throat. 'Let him go.' He cleared his throat again and spat out the paan juice and groaned once. I was about to jump in joy when he said. 'No. It will rain tonight.'

Mother looked at me, her lips twisted wryly. She stood there silently for a few minutes and then said softly, 'There's no sign of rain …'

The answer was a growl, 'I said no. It's cold in the south. It's raining in the hills.'

What was there to say? Mother looked at me helplessly, her eyes full, and returned to the kitchen.

I went to my room and picked up a book to read.

I could hear the calls outside. Then there was silence.

They would have started without me. Now they would be walking in the stream. They would be searching for owlets as they walked. Now the Kathakali would start. The music would swell. My breast was aflame.

At ten o'clock, I went to bed. Father at eleven. Within half an hour I could hear him snoring. I got up slowly and arranged a pillow, my school bag and a box on the bed, covered it with my blanket and silently walked towards the kitchen. I opened the door and stepped into the backyard. A cold current of wind blew towards the north, like a river. The mango tree in the north yard shrieked in the wind, 'Oye! Oye!'

I reached the temple premises. The sky was dark. Not a single star could be seen. When the eye got used to the dark, I could see the ground. I went down to the stream. A nearby mango tree was pregnant with the screaming of the wind, its dry leaves dropping like rain. In the stream, the water was knee-deep. It was pleasantly warm.

Once you crossed the stream, you entered the ripening rice fields. In the middle of the field was a broad path that led to Padacheri and Valiya Yela. Tripparappu is after those. I ran. At times, my feet sank into crab holes. In the moonlight, the stagnant water in the fields glinted like the sharpened edge of a scimitar. The frogs kept up a constant cacophony. We used to make frog cries by rubbing the eyes of coconut shells against each other.

When I reached Padacheri, I could hear the roar of the Tripparappu waterfall. Padacheri was asleep.

Darkness blanketed the trees and houses. A dog lifted his eyes and asked, 'Who?' His question woke up dozens of other sleeping dogs. But the first dog knew me. I walked slowly, looking at his eyes glowing like two fireflies in the dark.

By the time I reached Valiya Yela, I could hear the beat of the Kathakali drums. The very sound was festive, embodying the warm glow of lighted lamps, of crowds, of temple payasam, of *Thidambu*[15] and elephants, of bronze bells, of stone steps, of dew and the cackle of banyan leaves.

However, when I reached the Tripparappu temple yard, I was really taken aback. The yard was almost empty! Under a coconut tree, Gopalan the elephant was eating a palm frond disinterestedly. On the stage, the Kathakali performance continued lackadaisically to listless drums. In front of the stage, there were only ten people or so – old men. I couldn't see a single woman there. Behind the stage, in the light thrown by it, I could see the branches of the banyan tree. It swayed like one possessed, like a demon reaching out with powerful arms to grab the stage.

I sat down, a little apart from the spectators, on the stone steps. Who was on the stage? By his dress and red beard, I figured it was an *asura*. It must be Hiranya. I sat there, wide-eyed, watching his demonic demeanour. A young boy entered the stage. Except for a sacred lock, a *kutuma*, his head was covered in cloth to resemble a shaven head. A brave lad indeed! Hiranya's wicked expression, gestures and prancing did not frighten him. Hiranya reached out to grab the boy. He threatened to kill him. Tried to frighten him with his sharp teeth and nails.

I itched to pick up a stone and throw it at Hiranya's head. He should bleed. Most probably, under that crown, he would be bald. But my aim was bad. If only brother was here. He always found his mark. Suddenly, I wondered where he would be now. He wouldn't be travelling back by the river. In this wind, no one would travel by the river.

A heavy hand landed on my shoulder. Even before I could turn to see who it was, I realized it was Father's fevered hand.

'Come,' he said shortly, and started walking. I rose and followed him, like a sleepwalker. How did he realize that I had left? How did he realize where I was? Maybe I was dreaming.

The wind had died. It was cold. Stray droplets of rain fell on us. Father did not turn to look at me even once. I felt he was going to murder me. He would whip me as soon as we reached home. Once he began his beating, it would end only if someone intervened. He would beat me with whatever he found. Sometimes he pulled out the rod from the canvas of the easy chair to beat me. Why didn't I just run away? But to where? I could run away to Trivandrum. Over there, young boys could find work in hotels.

Still, I followed him like an obedient dog. The croaking of the frogs had become deafening. It sounded as noisy as a crowded marketplace. Father turned to a different path. He would not lose his way. Maybe he was taking me somewhere to kill me. He could take me to *Chudala Madan Kovil* and sacrifice me to the gods. He would slit my throat and wash Chudala Swami with my blood. There was a makeshift bridge that was made out of a single coconut trunk near the *Chudala Madan Kovil.* When the water in the stream rose, people would use this path. The brook below the bridge was full. It rushed, twisting and turning, thick as a python. The only thing you could hear in the dark was its rushing sound.

Father asked me to get on the bridge. In our village, everyone knew how to cross a bridge made of a single coconut tree trunk. Pregnant women, people carrying loads on their heads, old men and women – all treated it as a normal path. I was used to running across them, yet that night my legs shook. Father said, 'Get on.' I got on.

The coconut tree bridge swayed slightly. Below it, the maddened stream rushed past. I could feel my father's step behind me. My eyes dimmed. My legs felt numb. It would have been easy if there was a railing. However flimsy it was, it would have helped me balance. But …

Suddenly, my feet slipped. I felt my mind fall with it and shatter into a thousand pieces. That moment, Father placed his hand on my shoulder. My legs gained strength. I realized that it was my mind that had gained in strength. He pulled his hand away after that brief touch. I crossed the bridge with firm steps.

That time, Father did not whip me. Nor did he utter a word. I hung around for a while for the beating and then went off to sleep. Outside, it had started raining in earnest. That rain lasted for ten days. A torrent. Under the blanket, I felt the warmth of my father's hand on my shoulder again and again.

2

Nanjinadu – The Part of Kerala That Broke Off

I

Two Winds

Nanjinadu is a place where the sun blazes fiercely the entire day. But when it sets, you start wondering immediately if it might rain. During the day, the heat boils over and congeals in the yard like a solid, white wall. The next moment, without any warning, it grows dim. You notice it only because of the moving shadows.

The heat is stressful. You sweat. Your neck and armpits burn. You drink water. Yet, you are perpetually thirsty. Trees and plants stay motionless, in a stupor. Cattle cease flicking their ears and hold their heads low. Far away, over the top of Veli Hills, the sky is bathed in blue. From the emerald fields, fenced in by tall coconut trees, steam rises. Even the cranes abandon the fields and seek the shade on the banks.

The grip of the heat loosens a bit by the time the school bell rings and children spill out of classrooms. The tinkle of chatter, laughter and colour on tiny tongues. The shadows lengthen on the thorn fences and dusty lanes. Slowly, the cattle wake from their stupor. Their cry for water echoes everywhere. Birds stir, flap their wings and twitter. It's time for them to wake up from their siesta. A thought arises unbidden – life is sweet in spite of everything.

The people of Nanchinadu love their siestas. In every village, beneath the banyan trees, there are platforms made of cool smoothened stone. The Mootharamman shines have broad platforms polished with black oxide; gatehouses, where a weary traveller can rest and stone platforms in temples.

The eastern wind starts blowing then, almost reluctantly. Its caress as welcome as the touch of a cool young palm frond on sweaty skin, the touch of soft, young hair. On the ground, you hear the leaves stir. Dry leaves and stray bits of paper become animated. If you want to enjoy the eastern breeze, you have to mix it with the colours of a good Tamizh song – of Sirkazhi Govindarajan's, or Madurai Somu's '*chinnarinju penpole, chittade edayuduthi …*'

The eastern breeze blows till night. It brings with

it the salt and sultriness of the Kanyakumari seas. The fishermen's boats ride on it to reach the shore. A common question on everyone's tongue in the evening is: 'What is the catch today? What is the gift of the east?' Swordfish or sardine, mackerel or pipefish? Those who know the sea will tell you in advance that today it will be sardine. The eastern breeze smells of it.

The southern wind blows in the dark. When you wake up after a bout of sleep and step out of the house to urinate you will hear the coconut trees wail, their heads whirling as though possessed. In the moonlight, shadows cavort. Windows bang shut. Sleeping children start awake, mumble, turn in their beds and go back to sleep. In the kitchen, vessels clatter. On the table, the half-read magazine scatters. The southern wind is always cold – it has the chill of the mountains, the forests and the clouds. It carries the fragrance of champak flowers, or *kallipala* (dyer's oleander) flowers blooming somewhere in the Kaliyankattil forest. It carries the strains of southern ballads sung in far-off shrines to the beat of native fiddles – stories of Eravikuttipillai and of Thampi's, memories of yakshis and *neeli*s.

Nanchinadu lies in the middle of two winds – the challenging eastern wind and the comforting southern wind. The eastern carries ochre dust, while the southern wind brings vapour and the scent of wild leaves. In the June–July months of Aani and Aadi, the southern winds come carrying clouds. The clouds are thick and dark like buffaloes. They wrap Nanchinadu for days, and all you will hear is the sound of the rain. Pathways turn into rivulets; trees fold their wings and huddle; the submerged fields sparkle and stretch as far as the eye can see, the water ochre coloured, as though attired in red silk. Rivers flex their muscles, the rain-drenched walls stand thrilled. When the water drains, you can see the imprint of the waves on the soft sand.

The eastern wind blows in the month of *Aiparasi*, October–November, the season when the whole of Tamil Nadu is drenched with rain. The eastern rain comes like the waves of the sea, crashes loudly on the land and retreats. The next moment, the sky clears and it becomes bright again. From the eaves, water drops down like glowing glass beads. The leaves, pregnant with water, bow low and shed pearls. Once again, cloud waves gather in the east.

You should not get wet in the southern rain. It is cold and brings with it fevers and cholera. Getting wet in the eastern rain is delicious. The colour of the southern rain is blue while the eastern rain is pale yellow. If the south darkens, the rain will be a torrent; when the east darkens, you are merely drenched – so goes an old saying.

Nanchinadu, with its two rainy seasons, has some of the most fertile soil in South India. A land of three harvests, and of coconut, banana and rubber plantations. The very colour of Nanchinadu is green. The hills, mountains, the fields, the hedges, why, even the roofs are green.

It is the darling of two mothers.

II

Legends

The person behind the prosperity of this land is Marthanda Varma Kulasekhara Perumal, who ruled Travancore from 1729 to 1758 – the brave hero who lives on in local stories and legends. If you want to discover the condition of Nanchinadu before Marthanda Varma, you will have to search the folk songs of the land. Those songs – the *villupattu* and the village *kalipattu* – collected and published in Tamizh by Dr A.K. Perumal – paint a scary picture. Nanchinadu was the favourite hunting ground of Muslim rulers and Telugu-speaking Hindu chieftains. It was a rich granary without any protection. These songs are full of lamentations against the thieving *Tulukar* and *Vadukar* who stole entire harvests. To counter the attacks, after the harvest, the people of

Nanchinadu started mixing the harvested paddy with stones and burying it in the soil, or mixing it with ochre soil and building walls with it, or making them into big bricks and burying them. When the marauders came, the men would run away and hide in the mountains.

The thieves quickly found a solution. They would capture the women and take them as a bargaining chip. To get the women back you had to pay in gold and grain. To this day, the children of Nanchinadu play, singing:

> 'I'll give a pot of grain, let the girl go *Tuluka*.'
> 'For a pot of grain, *Tulukan* will not let the girl go.'
> 'I'll give two pots of grain, let the girl go *Tuluka*.'
> 'For two pots of grain, *Tulukan* will not let the girl go.'

Beyond all this were the regular murders and pilferage by the Maravar tribes from the Kalakkadu, Panakudi and Thenkasi regions. Even today, each family's lore has its own story of thievery and murder from those times. There is one in Mother's family as well. The Maravar from Kalakkadu raided their house and found only the womenfolk. They caught them and tied them to the tamarind trees around and hung grinding stones on their feet. When they opened the granary, they found paddy mixed liberally with stones, which they could not carry. They returned empty-handed, leaving the women hanging from the trees. Their backbones shattered from the weight of the stones; the women died, screaming in agony.

Marthanda Varma arrived as a strong leader of this leaderless land. He brought in line the tyrannical feudal lords, the Brahmin landlords and the temple authorities. He demarcated borders and gave laws. He built forts and created military encampments along the border. He built canals from the river Ponman and brought water to each corner of Nanchinadu. The water distribution system put in place during his reign survives to this day. In fact, there are people who claim that Marthanda Varma's story is the story of Nanchinadu.

An astonishing aside in the history of Travancore

Marthanda Varma had two strong lieutenants – Chief Minister Dalawa Ramaiah and Captain Benedict de Lannoy. Soon after he assumed power, Marthanda Varma travelled through his kingdom. While he was resting at the Vadiveeshwaram Temple, he saw that the lamps were about to go out. When he saw that there was hardly any oil in the lamps, he ordered that they be refilled. A young Brahmin boy from Madapalli ran up to do his bidding. He first lit another wick from the temple lamp and held it while filling the lamp with oil. What if the lamp went out while being filled with oil? The king liked his caution and took the boy with him. He educated him and appointed him first as an *adhikari*, an important official, and then as minister.

Dalawa Ramaiah became a wonder in Travancore history. He remained a bachelor. Bachelorhood among Brahmins, especially Iyers, was extremely rare in those days. If you did not have a son to perform the rites after your death, how could you attain Swarga, or Heaven? Neither was he a Sanyasi. It is said that after he passed away, a Nair woman arrived at the court from Mavelikkara and handed a cover that had been entrusted to her by the Dalawa. Inside was a palm leaf document written in the minister's hand stating that he had accepted her as his wife. Though a Brahmin, Ramaiah was not a priest. He belonged to a group known as Chozhiya Brahmins who had relocated to Travancore from Chozha Nadu (Ramaswamy also belongs to this group). Most of them settled down in Madapalli. It is doubtful if the Dalawa was even a strong believer in the faith he was born into. He was a Brahmin who picked up a sword and went to do battle. It is also unlikely that Marthanda Varma would have been able to consolidate his power in Travancore without his help. The Nambudiri overlords of the temples of Suchindram, Thiruvattar and Parashala had established independent principalities with the temple lands. Ramaiah was responsible for single-handedly driving them away. Those days, when fear and respect for the Brahmin community was at its peak, only another Brahmin would have been able to do it.

There is a story about Ramaiah defeating the Suchindram overlords. The king was returning home via Suchindram after praying at the temple at Nagarcoil. To prepare for his reception, he sent word to Suchindram through a messenger. To thumb their nose at him and to assert their power, the temple priests quickly locked up the temple and left. The king saw the locked temple and returned to Nagarcoil. An enraged Ramaiah took a small army and chased the entire priestly clan – the overlords of the temple – out of Travancore. They had never anticipated such an outcome!

A few years before this incident, Ramaiah had visited the Suchindram Temple. That time he was allowed to rest in the veranda of a Brahmin house known as Vattapalli Madom. They also gave him rice gruel with tamarind curry. Later, the people of Vattapalli Madom were ostracized by the other Nambudiris for hosting a man who was slightly lower than them in the caste heirarchy.

When Ramaiah returned to Suchindram to avenge the king's disgrace, he razed the Nambudiri houses to the ground and spared Vattapalli Madom. Recently, when I visited Suchindram with A.K. Perumal, a man pointed to a veranda and exclaimed, 'This is the veranda where Ramaiah rested.' According to records, Ramaiah's ancestors belonged to a village called Ervadi in Tamil Nadu. From there they came to Vadiveeshwaram in Nagarcoil, where they settled down.

Esthacius Benedict De Lennoy was twenty-seven years old when he reached Kulachil port on a ship. In the battle that was fought on 10 June 1741, he was defeated and captured. While he was in jail as a prisoner of war, Marthanda Varma used to visit him. The king wanted to know more about the rifle that belonged to the captain. A rare and unlikely friendship blossomed between these two very different men. De Lennoy faithfully served a land where he had no roots for thirty-seven years, fought battles for it and died there.

Olakal and *Sheelakal*

The army of Travancore was just a band of primitive people without much training. There was no standing army. When there was a war, the feudal lords quickly gathered a group of able-bodied men to serve the king.

It was De Lennoy who created a standing army and trained them. Even today, his trick to teach soldiers to march survives as a children's game. The soldiers were asked to tie a strip of palm leaf – *ola* – on one leg and a strip of cloth – *sheela* – on the other. A man would shout, '*olakal sheelakal*' and men would march in order – left, right. History states that once the soldiers of Travancore learned how to march to *olakal sheelakal*, they were able to defeat other Kerala princedoms. It eliminated the ubiquitous problem of falling down during hand-to-hand combat.

It was De Lennoy who also created strong stone fortresses in Aralvaymozhi, Kanyakumari and Udayagiri to protect Travancore. With these forts, De Lennoy was able to protect Nanchinadu from the marauders who came from beyond the mountains. In 1744, De Lennoy bought 150 guns and 200 pistols from the British army. This marked the beginning of the modernization of the Travancore army. He created a factory to make gunpowder near Padmanabhapuram – Marunnukottai – and made arrangements to cast cannons in Udayagiri. He built a navy made up of small, swift, seaworthy ships and expanded the seaports. He married twice. His eldest son, Johannes De Lennoy, died when he was nineteen while fighting Kalakattu Maravar who came to raid Travancore.

When I travel from Nagarcoil to Trivandrum, I look at my native land with immense pride. It is a land without hunger. If the district with the highest percentage of education in Tamil Nadu is Kanyakumari, in Kerala it is Trivandrum. Dams, fertile fields, plantations … the prosperity of this land is based on these three features. These in turn owe their existence to Marthanda Varma and his two friends. Marthanda Varma is the epitome of the Malayalee's ability to exploit opportunities and overcome challenges. It is the same fascination that Marthanda Varma experienced 250 years ago when he first saw De Lennoy's gun that drives the Malayalee today to explore new fields and pursue adventures.

Dalawa Ramaiah represented the passion and strength of Tamizh, the fountainhead of Malayalam. His entire life he fought for a land that wasn't his own. The Malayalam land occupies a very special place in the heart of the Tamil people. This has been so from time immemorial and continues to this day. I have noticed this many a time, and it never fails to surprise me. You can see this love in Subramania Bharathi and in V.V. Subramaniam Aiyar. Manonmaniyam Sundaram Pillai shared it. Sundara Ramaswamy and Jayakanthan, too. Devadevan, Vannadasan and Yuvan have expressed it. Maybe it is because of the ubiquitous presence of old

Tamizh words in Malayalam, or maybe because old Tamizh rituals and practices survive in the Malayalee to this day.

The contribution of the Tamizh people in establishing modern Travancore is considerable. The first Dalawa Arumukam Pillai, his trusted friend Kumara Swamy Pillai, Sthanumalayan Nadar (Marayyan) who saved Marthanda Varma's life … the list is long, including Sir C.P. Ramaswamy Iyer, who is remembered by the people of southern Travancore to this day. In the modern revolutionary history of Kerala, Iyer is remembered for many other things, but he is the one who laid the economic foundation for Travancore, which survives even today. The Nagarcoil–Trivandrum highway rests on the cement road that Iyer built. For our roads, irrigation and drinking water, we have to thank Iyer's foresight and planning.

De Lennoy is not a rarity. If we consider modern Indian history, we can recognize one thing – the places that came into contact with European culture had a head start in development, education and social awakening. Travancore was a place that Europeans loved. Missionaries from St Xavier lived and worked here. They played a role in developing the reach of education and fought to ensure the rights of the people, including the right of lower-caste women to cover their breasts. It was served by great Europeans from Rinkle de Nambé to Charles Mead. The list includes the doctor in Neyyoor, Dr Somerville, to Reverend Thombar.

When I talk of Kerala, I talk about a big part of the history of my land. I do not get any of my history from books or etchings. I have wandered in every nook and cranny of this land. I have visited temples and churches, I have studied people's lifestyles and I can reproduce their dialect perfectly. And although I have written 3,000 pages about this land, the unspoken is substantial. It needs to be written.

III

The Malayalee Is Ashamed of His Dialect

I had gone to Trivandrum to attend the wedding of a relative. From the moment I crossed the threshold to the venue, I began to feel suffocated.

'Has brother-in-law arrived?' I asked a woman.

'*Elya* ... No,' she said in a strange dialect.

Who is this lady from Valluvanad? I wondered. When I inquired where she was from, she said Parashala!

Soon enough it was evident that all the women were speaking in the same strange dialect. I could speak the beautiful Tamizh of Thanjavur, courtsey of my wife, and the dialect of Travancore, which I learnt from the women in my house. I began to feel like a stranger. That's when I spied the grandmother, sitting alone on a bench chewing paan. I walked up to her.

'How are things, Ammachi?'[1] I asked.

'Just carrying on. At least you speak our language. Do say something,' she pleaded. She, too, was feeling suffocated without a soul to speak to.

'These women learn this dialect watching TV serials. I wish I would die after understanding their language!' Her voice was scornful.

A generation is going to pass away holding their language close to their breast. Today, no one likes to speak in the Travancore dialect. It is a language that is looked down upon as low class. It can be used for comedies. When Mammooty comes on screen, one-eyed and wearing a fluorescent pink shirt and speaks in this dialect, people roar with laughter. For those belonging to high culture, it is Valluvanad dialect. If you say '*Ooh*', people will laugh; you have to say '*Ovu*' to make it sound sweet. In the last half-century, this is one of the major cultural shifts that has happened in Kerala.

The Tamil actor Arya is a close friend of mine. He is a Mappila named Emshad, whose family were originally from Calicut. His family had settled in Chennai a generation ago. Although his bread and butter is the Tamizh language, at home he consciously chose to speak in Malayalam – the original Malayalam spoken in Calicut. But if you try to speak that in Calicut, it will not work. The Valluvanadan dialect has colonized their dialect, too. When I say Valluvanadan dialect, it is a euphemism. In reality, it is the language of the Valluvanad Nambudiris. The so-called cultured people speak that language in an attempt to partake of Nambudiri superiority!

B-grade Malayalam movies and serials use print language as the spoken language. I wonder if this practice is prevalent in any other Indian language. 'Chadrashekaran will not rest till he achieves it. Chadrashekaran will never give up.' This dialogue is spoken by none other than Chandrashekaran himself! If it is a matter of love, the language becomes even more pompous. 'All that I desire from you is a peacock feather to keep in the silver jewel box of my heart … that … that alone … I desire from you.' The writers of film songs are no better. They use strange words, and insert normal Malayalam words only here and there.

I doubt if anywhere else in India you would find a group of people who hate the very foundation of their culture. The Malayalee is afraid of his dialect. He hides it. He considers it unworthy, belonging to low culture. After the language of the press, what he values next is the language of the Nambudiris. In TV interviews, many actresses inadvertently slip into their dialect. But no actress will ever speak the dialect of Cannanore or Trivandrum. I have often wondered about the filter that transforms one's mother tongue into an alien one.

I remember discussing this issue with P.K. Balakrishnan many years ago. As usual, he launched into a long monologue. He began with a quip, 'Doesn't your guru speak the Valluvanadan dialect?' He was referring to Atoor Ravi Varma.

'That's the language of the place he was born,' I answered.

'You have to take into account a few things that happened when Kerala was born,' Balakrishnan continued. 'Travancore was divided. Half of it became part of Tamil Nadu. With that, the entity – Travancore – ceased to exist. Travancore has very little significance in the cultural context of Kerala today. If you look back at the division, you will realize that it was a natural process. The idiotic political class here considered the Tamizhan as the other. They suppressed them. When they demanded their rights, they were faced with weapons. None of them recognized that the culture of Travancore partakes of both Malayalam and Tamizh culture. Most of them were votaries of the stinking caste hierarchies.'

Signs of Feudalism

'Kerala created its own cultural identity through Vallathol, E.M.S., etc.,' Balakrishnan explained. 'They failed to imagine a dialogic culture that draws on diverse, multiple strands. Instead, they had a monolithic culture in mind. A culture with a single, unifying focus. They delved into the past in search of it. They reached Ezhuthachan and Sanskrit grammar. That is how all our cultural signs became extensions of feudal lifestyles. This marks the beginning of the Malayalee's insane quest for high culture.'

I remember Balakrishnan mentioning two things, almost to himself. 'There is an aspect that you can see across India. Almost all localized history begins with the Bhakti movement or, if it does not, there is a tendency to see it as such. There appears to be a hidden political agenda behind E.M.S. going back to Ezhuthachan in history and beginning with him. In my opinion, you should never determine a nation's culture based on its past. The more you travel back, the definition of culture becomes more backward-looking and insular. You have to determine culture from the point where you stand, from the time in which you exist, looking forward. Culture is not a decorative flower vase. It is a tool like a knife, a spatula or a key.'

Almost twenty years have passed since we had that conversation. I am yet to fully grasp the import of what Balakrishnan said. (The only thing I remember distinctly is his sharp reprimanding of E.M.S.) When I look back, I can clearly see that Kerala has decoupled itself from its original culture and has travelled a long way away from it. The distance between Thiruvattar and Trivandrum is now as long as the distance from Thiruvattar to Thrissur.

IV

The Trivandrum that Has Moved Away

When I was a young boy, Trivandrum was very close. It is not a euphemism. It is the truth. There were buses to Trivandrum from the interior villages that traversed the mountain roads. Today, they are no longer there, nor do people from the interior visit Trivandrum as often.

Those days, the last bus from Trivandrum would reach our village square at eleven in the night. The driver and the conductor would park the vehicle and retire to Achutan's tea shop. They would drink arrack and go to sleep. It was not uncommon for drivers who ran the same route for over a year to have a mistress in the place. The driver and conductor would get up early in the morning and bathe in the clear waters of the Vayambadi brook. Then they would pray at the small roadside shrine to Krishna and receive the prasad – tulsi leaves and sandalwood paste. By five-thirty, they would be sitting in the bus sounding the horn. The bus would leave only after half an hour. Till then they would keep honking. Most of the travellers left their house only when they heard the horn. People from remote corners, who wished to travel by this bus, would have arrived the night before. They slept on the *thinnai*s in front of the shops, and would be sitting inside the bus even before the conductor arrived.

Girl, Haven't You Gone to See the Palace Yet?

Father would go to Trivandrum at least twice a month. Those days, people travelled all the way to Trivandrum to buy clothes and gold. People were satisfied only if they wandered around in the terrible heat, ate a couple of banana fritters and bought their goods from Aryashala – the main market. They would worship at the Padmanabhaswamy Temple, or if that didn't work out, at least at the one at Pazhavangadi. Only then would they hurry to catch the last bus home. Bigger weddings happened only in Trivandrum. Women would take out their silk and *neriyathu*[2] from wooden chests where they had been stored with dried *thazhampoo* – the fragrant screwpine flower. Children would wear shirts that had been carefully folded and kept under the pillow to make them look ironed. On those days, when there was a marriage or a festival, the bus would be full. Sometimes, the travellers would become sick and throw up, especially while driving downhill, where the road twisted and turned.

Those who were newly married were expected to go and visit Trivandrum, see the palace and the zoo there and then watch a movie. Matriarchs would pester the new bride, 'Girl, haven't you gone to see the palace yet?' I remember going on one such visit with a newly married couple to watch *Pani Theerata Veedu*, since custom demanded that they tag a naïve young boy along to keep away the evil eye. When I think back on this, my breath stops. Imagine a newly married couple from an interior village wearing a hundred sovereigns of gold wandering on the busy city roads of Trivandrum!

The people of Trivandrum, who lived under the benevolent eye of the Maharaja, considered the people of South Travancore gormless. If you consider my father and his ilk, to an extent it was true. The people of Trivandrum have a lot of humorous stories to tell about the people of Nanchinadu. Once a group of people from Nanchinadu went to the common dining hall to have their lunch. Soon a fight broke out between them and another group. In anger, the first group lifted a guy and threw him into the *uruli*[3] which held the piping hot payasam. Only then did they realize that in their haste they had grabbed the wrong man. He was in fact a part of their own group! So they immediately lifted him out of the uruli and threw him into the uruli in which the buttermilk was kept, thus saving his life!

Scenes from Trivandrum

There are even more stories about the matriarchs who visited Trivandrum with their husbands. When one of these women saw a statue near Victoria Hall, she wondered aloud, 'Who made this? Who made it stand like this?' In fact, there was a ballad about a matriarch who came to visit Trivandrum. You could buy a copy of the ballad for two annas.[4] I have read it myself.

It is about a couple who visited Trivandrum. Those days, the bus stop was at Aryashala. As soon as they alighted, the couple went to an eatery where they had gruel. They had also bought jackfruit *aviyal* for two *chuckram*[5] to eat with the gruel. But the aviyal had gone bad. The lady could not stomach it. Traumatized, she hardly saw the city sights. Whenever her husband pointed out the sights to her, 'Look woman, the clock tower says twelve-thirty,' she would repeat this refrain:

The jackfruit aviyal was rotten,
My two chuckram were stolen.

The story goes that when another lady saw the long sword that belonged to the Maharaja at the Palace Museum, she exclaimed, 'Goodness, how can the Maharaja wield such a heavy sword? Can't the Nair chieftains tie up those he wanted killed and bring them in front of him?' The matriarchs of Nanchinadu were loyal to the king. They always boasted about their connections, imaginary or otherwise, with the royal household. 'Our mother's great-uncle's eldest sister's brother-in-law was the supplier of jaggery for the Palace,' so went the boast, or something in a similar vein. Until about twenty-five years ago, it was common to see in wedding invitations and in newspaper advertisements – 'N. Azhakappan Pilla, lentil supplier for the Palace', or descriptions of a similar kind.

Almost every house had a picture of Swati Thirunal in his feathered, bejewelled crown, looking sideways at you. There was one in our house as well – a colour portrait. I have often wondered whether that picture was taken when the king looked up in shock when he heard from Sardar Patel's emissary that he was no longer king. Though Father was employed by the government of Tamil Nadu, his loyalty was always to the other side. Every year, he attended the temple festival. People would start arriving at our place the day before. Most of them were elderly Nairs. Some of them were Vellalas. There was one Potti and one Kaipalli. There would also be a couple of Peruvattanmar[6] (Nadar landlords) – Father's friends. They would arrive before lunch. The lunch on that day would be elaborate. Kheer would be served. After lunch and a brief rest, they would bathe, change into festive clothes and pray at the temple. Then the whole party would leave for Trivandrum by bus.

During the entire journey they would wax eloquent on the king, exaggerating the superiority of his rule and his many admirable qualities. Sometimes, they were outright lies. How in the Thiruvattar Temple the massive decorative dome could not be lifted even by three hundred men and five elephants. But when the King merely touched it, it went up like a dream. How the Thiruvattar Temple elephant, Keshavan, walked all the way to Trivandrum on his own for the festival. How he ran away crying when the Maharaja passed away. The group would go to the Kizhakekotta (East Fort) and stay at some Potti Madom – a traditional guesthouse. They would bathe and worship at the Padmanabhaswamy Temple. They would not sleep that night. They traded gossip and stories over paan. Early morning, before the sun rose, they would stand on the road waiting for the king. The king would walk down the road, freshly bathed, a holy tilak on his forehead, wearing a simple dhoti with a gold border and carrying the ceremonial sword. They would watch him, their hearts aflame, their eyes full of happy tears!

Like a Walking Flame

'These days, people claim that the Maharaja is also human, no? Can those people walk like him? That grandeur, that majesty!' For six months at least after their visit to Trivandrum people would keep marvelling: 'He was like a walking flame! When the right person rules, the country will prosper. What else is there to say?' Once I, too, went with them. I was with Father when I saw the king worshipping at a temple there. The guards chased us away into a corner. People were huddled there like so many cattle. Every man had his palms folded in prayer. They were worshipping the king. The Tamilians who came from outside Kerala looked at the sight, astounded. 'Irreverent wretches,' Father said with feeling. The next day, when I saw the king walking with his upheld sword, I was afraid he would hurt himself. He looked like a timid, affectionate Malayalam schoolteacher, or maybe a music teacher. When I told that to Mother, she laughed so hard that her breath caught in her throat.

Thirty-five years have passed since then. I still hear Father's sentiments expressed in different tongues. Manikantan's tea shop is opposite our office. It is a thatched structure. Most of his customers are plantain farmers from the interior. After three o'clock, old Ayyappan Pilla saunters in. He is over ninety. He will stand perplexed on this side of the national highway, peering through his thick spectacles at the rushing vehicles. Once he manages to cross the road and find his usual place on the wooden bench, he begins to unwind. All the energy that was once in his body is now concentrated in his tongue. He has a large, admiring audience, including me. Ayyappan's philosophy has a logic of its own. Today's topic is the current lack of rain.

'How will there be rain? These days, we are selling rain, no? Will any mother suffer if her breast milk is sold?'

Ayyappan is talking in Tamizh. Sometimes a Malayalam word creeps in.

'Who sells rainwater?' I ask innocently.

'How do you think all this farming works, son? It is rain. Coconut, bananas, rubber … it's all rain. Mother Nature provides rain to feed her children so that they can flourish. Instead, we grow stuff to sell. Lord Ayyappa hates rubber. Chentuluvan detests bananas. Those bananas look like newly birthed babies. It is not for our consumption. It is for the white man. The white man is a devil who will eat even a baby, raw.'

Ayyappan is referring to cash crops. 'You can farm rice, you can farm plantains, can you farm cash? Will Mandakkattamma tolerate it if you farm cash?'

'But haven't the rains failed earlier as well?' I counter.

'Of course. The rain used to be pissed off earlier as well. But then there were responsible people to question our actions and make amends for them. Children, listen, this happened long ago. Those days, I was very young, very strong. That was when the southern rain failed. "If the southern rain fails, the eastern will follow suit", so goes an old saying. Nanchinadu was in distress. People were starving. They ate roasted jackfruit seeds and yam in a vain attempt to assuage their hunger. They got mouth ulcers and diarrhoea after eating those. The very young and the very old started dying. The elders belonging to the Parakkapidaka Pillais decided to go to Trivandrum to do something about it. They collected money – four *panam* per person – to procure the royal offering. It consisted of the usual stuff – rice, jaggery, plantains, tobacco. They set off in a procession of ten bullock carts to the palace to see the Maharaja. The Maharaja agreed to meet them. We didn't know any of this. We youngsters wandered the length and breadth of the land collecting what little grain was left to make gruel for the people. Fed the young some thin gruel. Someone said, "If you make an effigy of *Kodumpavi* – heinous sins – and burn it as an offering, it will rain." It was a common practice among the people of Tamil Nadu. We created a Kodumpavi kolam with hay and rattan – a figure with horns and huge ears. We planned to burn him in the temple yard of Koonankani Shastavu. We gathered the villagers, beating tin drums. All of them congregated and started ritually abusing the Kodumpavi. We were about to burn him.'

The Amazing Grace That Ruled over Us

'That's when we heard the beating of drums on the Nagarcoil road. Some of us ran to check what it was. There were two drummers, around eight people carrying spears, a few lords and a young girl wearing a turban on a pure white horse. People ran out to see the girl on the horse. When the horse came closer, it was evident that it wasn't a girl but a fair young man. He was wearing a silk blouse and dhoti; in his ears he wore ruby studs and around his neck a long string of pearls. Someone whispered, "It is the Maharaja!"

'We had never laid our eyes on the Maharaja. How can commoners like us see the king? We could not take our eyes from his face. He was glowing! Our eyes could barely take it in. The king was moving ahead. Suddenly, I recognized that the people from Parakkapidaka had invited him. Were his blessed feet going to touch our land as well? I looked at the local overlords. They stood there as one, palms folded in prayer, happy tears streaming from their eyes!

'Those days I was only a local scamp, but I didn't hesitate. Without bothering about his bodyguards, I jumped in front of the Maharaja and cried, "Beloved lord, if you want to kill me, please do, but please place your blessed feet on our land. Please bless our land." A spear-bearing Nair lunged forward, but the Maharaja prevented him with a quick gesture. "I will. What is the problem in that?" he said, smiling innocently like a child.

'He came to the Shastavu Temple. Those days, the temple looked very different. It had mud walls and a floor plastered with cow dung. The Maharaja sat on the thinnai. Without thinking, I quickly clambered up a coconut tree and cut down a bunch of tender coconuts. I promptly cut off the top of one and offered it to the king. He accepted the tender coconut from my hands and drank from it. The people were still crying.

'The Maharaja pointed to the straw figure and asked me, "What is that?"

'"It's *Kodumpavi.* We are going to burn it," I replied.

'"Don't do that. Poor thing! What did it do to you?" he said, smiling.

'He got up and blessed us, "May you prosper."

'The Maharaja got on his horse and left. We followed him, chanting prayers. When we reached the outskirts, we were asked to return. We returned as though celebrating a great victory.

'On the way, I stopped at Madan Chettiar's shop. I told him, "Chettiar, today is the day when the feet of the Maharaja blessed our land. Today, everyone should have kheer. I need rice and jaggery. In return, you can take all the land that belongs to me and my family."

'"Take," said Chettiar. We made kheer with rice, jaggery and coconut in the temple yard itself. We fashioned cups with palm leaves and served everyone. Hardly had we finished when a cool wind began to blow from the south. The wind foretold what was to come. People began singing and dancing with joy. It started raining. It rained all night. Shivering wet, I went home. It rained the whole morning, too. The over-abundant rain filled the parched land.

'Those were the days,' Ayyappan said. 'What do you know about the southern rain? It is the gift from Lord Padmanabhaswamy. It obeys the Padmanabha *dasan*.[7] These are things that our forefathers told us. This land remained fertile because of the sanctity of our kings. This green is their blessing.'

V

Sinned Women

'*Ettu Kutta Thamburante Katha*' is one of the folk songs of Nanchinadu that is yet to be published. It means 'The Story of the Eight Lords'. This song is sung in the Mootharamman kovils of Nanchinadu and has been transmitted orally. In this you can find an account of Marthanda Varma defeating the powerful Ettuveettil Pillamar and how he annihilated their families through the *thurakayattuka* of their womenfolk – literally 'abandon them on the wharf'.

Marthanda Varma defeated and killed Ettuveettil Pillamar. But he could not kill the womenfolk because it was against dharma. He did not want to exile them either because the children born to these women could come back and claim their land.[8] So he decided to destroy their caste and hit upon *Thurakayattal* as the solution. He imprisoned all the womenfolk of the Ettuveettil Pillamar. They were chained to an elephant and dragged to the Muttam beach in Kanyakumari, where they were auctioned off to the fishermen. It is said that the Portuguese also bought a considerable number of them to keep as slaves.

The girls in kachamundu
The girls in kannadimundu
Were bought by the mukkuvas
Auctioned for a hundred
And the young ones
Auctioned for a hundred

So goes the song of '*Ettu Kutta Thamburante Katha*'. A.K. Perumal deduces that the event mentioned in the song may have happened in 1734.

The picture of Marthanda Varma you get from the folk songs of Nanchinadu is quite different from the one you get from C.V. Raman Pillai's novel.[9] The human tongue is not subservient to any power on earth. The pre-eminence of the Thampis and the cruelty of Varma are etched forever in these songs, which have passed from tongue to tongue down the generations. My neighbour, the historian Dr Trivikraman Thampi, took the initiative to print the song '*Thampimar Kathai*'. It is a song that celebrates the valour of Pappu Thampi and Raman Thampi. You will find the Thampis glorified in many folk songs that A.K. Perumal has collected too. The stories that my aunt narrated of Marthanda Varma as I was growing up, were of a man who was cursed by women.

I still remember my aunt's teary eyes as she told us the stories. On hot summer evenings, we would sit on the cow dung-smeared floor behind the kitchen and she would tell the stories to eager kids. The women who fell to the ground unable to bear the weight of the iron chains, the sword-bearing guards who lashed them with whips made of buffalo skin to make them move faster, the elephants that dragged them to the beach, the fair faces of women wet with tears and blood, their hair undone, the bits of dirt and leaves that got caught in their long tresses, their torn clothes coming loose and trailing on the ground. They wailed, calling upon goddesses and their ancestors to save them. Some of the women merely moved their hands in supplication. They had lost their voices, having cried and cried in vain. Men and women who had gathered on the streets to watch stood shocked, their hands on their breasts, their eyes full of tears. Powerful images. As we listened to her, the sound of vessels from the kitchen would sound like the clanging of iron chains and a tremor would pass down our spines.

Those days, in many houses, the older women who passed away returned. They would possess the young virgins in their own families. When we heard that Meenakshi Akkan of Arapura Veetil had been visited by one such grandmother, we ran to see her. Her uncle beat us and chased us away. We climbed a mango tree growing nearby, clambered into the attic and went down the stairs to see her. She was sitting in her room. From the way she sat, it was evident that it wasn't her. Her hair was undone. She crouched in a corner, crying, her knees drawn up to her chest. Her eyes were red from the constant crying. She was mumbling something. It was not clear what she was trying to say. The room was full of womenfolk from the neighbouring houses. They stared at her, holding their chins in surprise and shock. The uncle came up and spoke harshly to the women. 'Enough! Leave! She is not for your entertainment. She is a girl who has to be married off.' The women looked embarrassed. They did not utter a word.

When she heard her uncle's voice, the girl lifted her head and pleaded with outstretched hands. 'Son, Mother is hungry. Give me some water, child. Mother will die of thirst.' What astounded me was her voice. The voice that emanated from her throat was one I had never heard. It belonged to a very old woman.

'Hold your tongue, you wretch. Who invited you here?' Uncle shouted.

'Son, please don't scold me. Where else will I go? Who else do I have? I came here to see you all.' Akkan started crying, in a different voice.

'Okay. Now that you have seen us, leave. She is a girl who has to be married off. Don't spoil her.'

Akkan rocked back and forth, crying. 'Son, Mother is hungry. Mother is very thirsty.'

This was what she had been mumbling. She had an insatiable hunger and unquenchable thirst. People said she was the ghost of a woman who had been auctioned off at Muttam beach. She had died somewhere and had never received any death rites. No *pindam* – ceremonial rice – was offered to her, nor water. Now she wanders, ever hungry and thirsty. Many houses were visited by such ammachis. No one knows who they were. No one knows what to do. The only thing you could do was to make an offering to Umminithanka, who died horribly after her tongue was ripped out and she turned into a yakshi and lived in Melekkadu.

Before the woman who possessed Akkan departed, she cried horribly, 'I'm leaving, son.'

Akkan sat up and drank two full pots of water. She did not remember a thing!

The Travancore kingdom is built upon sins committed on women. The history of Marthanda Varma is also interesting for another reason. Pappu Thampi and Raman Thampi are in fact the sons of Raja Rama Varma. Marthanda Varma was the nephew. He claimed the throne on the strength of the matriarchal system by which land and power passed through the female line. But it was during his reign that women in Travancore started losing their prestige and power. This was because Marthanda Varma centralized power in his hands by undermining the local chieftains. These feudal lords who followed a matriarchal system lost their significance. His was a reign when power ceased to be associated not with custom but instead with weapons.

The story of South Travancore that I remember is one of the gradual devaluation of women. I know matriarchs who transacted business and managed farms, who held entire families together and looked after them. In some households, the matriarch had two husbands. I even knew an august lady who had three husbands. By the time of my mother's generation, landownership and the control of property had passed on to men, and women became slaves of their families. Confined within the four walls of the house, they meekly suffered the mental and physical abuse thrust on them and cried in the dark. They tearfully brought up their children and, when the children grew up, had to suffer their abuse as well. They died … their tears dried up by then from the incessant crying. My mother has three sisters. All three of them had stories similar to my mother's. Nanchinadu grew roots and branches on the sins committed on women and laughed in exultation.

While I was working in Kasaragod, people there used to be shocked at the enormous amounts given as dowry in Trivandrum. Even a lower-division clerk could demand lakhs of rupees, a hundred sovereigns, household goods, a scooter, … Once, my friend, Rasak Kuttikakam, remarked sarcastically, 'Friend, in your land, the most expensive thing appears to be a penis. How do you travel around without a care with such valuable goods?' When I see women exhibiting the value of their purchases, in the form of gold worn on their bodies, I remember my grandmother. She only wore a simple, white, two-piece saree. She did not wear any ornaments other than the heavy studs in her ears. 'Looks like a halter on a buffalo!' – that was her opinion of women wearing gold chains.

Recently, my friend, the poet, M.Yuvan, told me, 'Earlier, when we thought about Kerala, it was the image of coconut trees that jumped to the mind, these days it is of women modelling gold. The girls stand smiling, their bodies covered in ugly ornaments resembling crabs and snails.'

'The girls are for sale,' I said. 'They are the commodities in the most lucrative trade that exists currently in Kerala.'

VI

The South Wind Cheated

When I asked Ayyappan what had happened to Nanchinadu over the last twenty-five years, his response was brief – 'The south wind cheated.' When it starts raining in Kerala in June, it no longer rains in Nanchinadu. The reason, according to environmentalists, is the total destruction of the thick rainforest that covered the mountain ranges from Nedumangad to

Boothapandi. When the pattern of rain changed, the farming pattern and even the food habits of the people changed. 'What makes Nanchinadu, Nanchinadu is the rain that it gets in the Aani–Aadi months of June–July. The British rulers had tried to coax the Aadi rain beyond the Aralvaymozhi Ghats. It didn't work. Why? It is the gift of Lord Padmanabhaswamy,' Ayyappan was certain. For many years now, Aadi rain no longer blesses this land. Instead, the cold wind blows fiercely. The companies grab its speed with windmills and turn it into electricity. The windmills cover the hills from Nanchinadu to the valley beyond.

The beauty of South Travancore lies in its lakes and ponds. 'Between the tanks there are fields. That's what you see here,' said one of my friends when he first visited. The sea is close, so the water from the mountains can quickly wash into it. That must be the reason why our ancestors were so diligent about digging so many tanks. The only other place where I have seen so many tanks and ponds is lower Thanjavur, my wife's native place. Over there it is difficult to decipher where the tanks end and the paddy fields begin.

Most of the tanks in Nanchinadu were dug during the time of the Cholas and are named after Chola kings and queens. Many stone engravings dating to the period have been found here. They detail how the water in the tanks should be distributed. It is evident that the water system that exists in Nanchinadu today was designed during that period, according to the Chola custom. The Cholas ruled Nanchinadu for three hundred years. This period was followed by one of lawlessness. It was brought to an end with the arrival of Marthanda Varma.

Both Marthanda Varma and the Venad kings who succeeded him had many more ponds dug – often as many as fifty a year. From Boothapandi to Kanyakumari, and from there to Kaliyikavila, there are ponds around the base of the mountains. If you examine the famous Mudaliar documents, all you can see are records of ponds to be dug. If a king fell ill, or a queen had a nightmare, the solution was to dig a pond. If a royal couple visited a place, a tank was built there to commemorate the visit. If a defeated foe's house was razed to the ground, a tank was built in its place as a kind of atonement for the destruction.

I can say with certainty that the most prevalent 'building activity' in the last fifty years in Kanyakumari district has been the filling up of these ponds and tanks with soil. Almost all public buildings in Nagarcoil stand on sites where waterbodies once existed. Recently, the authorities drained a large pond and built a bus stop in its place. Next, they are going to fill up another large Chola-era tank, to build a new collectorate there. They also have plans to build a new railway station after filling up the Parashery Kulam, another large tank. A nearby tank has already been filled to build quarters for government staff. The goal of the Nagarcoil municipality appears to be to drain at least one water tank a year. A similar situation exists in all the small towns. The tanks on farmlands are filled up by individuals who want to convert the tank into farms or housing plots. A study conducted by the Vivekananda Study Centre proves that in just a decade, the number of ponds and tanks in the region has halved. It only needs another ten years to eliminate the remaining water tanks. With that, the Nanchinadu that existed before the Cholas will return.

The water that Nanchinadu gets these days comes from the heavy eastern monsoon that we receive every alternate year. Generally, Tamil Nadu receives rain when there is a combination of a depression and the east wind. The rain that fills the sky and the land lashes everything in its path. That rain comes straight here as well. Banana trees snap and keel over, the banks of the paddy farms breach and the water drains away; the water swells the rivers and they rush in a mad torrent towards the sea. A mere three months later, people start struggling for drinking water. Today, even before the onset of summer, the administrative bodies in Nagercoil issue warnings. Nagercoil receives water from an ancient earthfill dam built long ago by the visionary Sir C.P., who built it for the people of Nagercoil when it was still a small town. Even that has dried up. The Pechiparai Dam, neglected for more than fifty years without desilting, is also drying up. The groundwater here has receded as deep as *pathal*!

The hallmark of Tamil Nadu are the ubiquitous plastic pots. Every month, on every street, you can see, queued up in front of the public taps, large numbers of plastic pots in ugly colours with dark, gaping mouths. When I was a young boy travelling through Tirunelveli and Kovilpetti, I had hated the silent cry of these pots. I had sympathized with the people carrying water pots on cycles, on their shoulders, on waists and on their heads, desperately running on the streets after water. Today, Nanchinadu is full of plastic pots. Yesterday, I saw a truck pass by. It was going to Trivandrum. It had packets of plastic pots. These days, all over Kerala, in the months of April and May, all you can see are plastic pots in colours that appear as though they are burning in the summer sun!

VII

The Writers of Nanchinadu

In Nanchinadu there is a village called Azhikiya Pandiyapuram. A Shaiva Vellala family belonging to this village had been conferred the title of Mudaliar during the time of the Cholas. This family was in charge of the civil administration in Nanchinadu. They collected taxes, mediated and resolved civil cases and oversaw the distribution of water resources. When Nanchinadu became part of Venad, the Mudaliars continued to be in charge of the local administration. This state of affairs continued till the arrival of the British.

The house of the Mudaliars in Azhikiya Pandiyapuram had a collection of administrative records written on palm leaves for the past four hundred years. Known as the 'Mudaliar palm leaves' in Tamil, these records were studied and published by the poet and researcher 'Kavimani' Desika Nayakam Pillai. Although many of these records were later handed over to the Government of Kerala, they have not been studied extensively. They lie forgotten in some dusty corner in the government archives. This year, A.K. Perumal has published these documents in Tamil as *Mudaliar Oolachuvadikal* and it can authoritatively impact the study of the history of Travancore.

When A.K. Perumal came to visit me at home I inquired, 'Why is it that these valuable documents are completely overlooked in Kerala?' According to Perumal, there are two reasons for this negligence: 'Firstly, in today's cultural identity of Kerala, Travancore has very little significance. There is hardly any significant writer or researcher from Travancore. Hence, there is very little research on the region. Secondly, South Travancore is a limb that has fallen off from Travancore. In this past half-century they have forgotten its existence. The people there can hardly comprehend the cultural significance of South Travancore. Let me give you an example. The *Dictionary of Kerala Folklore* is a massive tome, compiled by M.V. Vishnunamboothiri. The majority of the entries in it are from North and Central Kerala. There is very little contribution to it from South Travancore.'

When I read the Mudaliar documents, I felt that there could be one more reason for this neglect. The descriptions in the documents might go against the grain of the current 'historical' research of the Malayalee. In most of the studies that I read today, I find that the Malayalee is more interested in recreating the 'ancient' and 'glorious' history of Kerala. In the Mudaliar documents, the Maharaja is constantly negotiating with the Vellala farmers in Nanchinadu. They get upset with him and flee as a body to Tirunelveli. The Maharaja comes down to Nanchinadu, stays in the Kottaru Palace and sends an emissary to them. When the farmers return, he begs their forgiveness and requests them to cultivate the lands. In one of the letters sent to the Mudaliars pleading with them to give him grain, the king writes, 'To meet the expenses of the palace, I look to your generosity.' When we enter the portals of history, what we witness is magnificent human drama. The researchers in Kerala go there expecting images that reiterate their constructions of Nair–Nambudiri superiority and Kerala nationalism.

How many distinguished writers have emerged from the Travancore region in the last fifty years? In my reading, there hasn't been any significant writers after C.V. Ramanpillai. Nor is there a work that vividly presents the story of any part of Travancore. I ruminated on the reasons behind this, and this is what I feel:

In the olden days, Travancore had a distinct identity and its source was South Travancore. One can illustrate this with just C.V. Ramanpillai's novels. They are imbued with the strong colours of Tamizh culture. Many of his memorable characters are, in fact, Tamilians. The geography that he describes so vividly is mostly South Travancore. Today these regions are all part of Tamil Nadu. When South Travancore was severed from North Travancore, the latter lost its identity.

However, the part of Kerala that dropped on Tamil soil did not lose its individuality and retains it to this day. The significance of this tiny geographical space in Tamil literature and culture is, indeed, immense. Early writers – Manonmaniam Sundaram Pillai, Kavimani Desigavinayagam Pillai, S. Vaiyapuri Pillai, K.N. Sivaraja Pillai and Vidhvan Lakhshanapillai, set the tone of modern Tamil literature; Sundaraswami, Krishnan Nambi, Nakulan, Neela Padmanabhan, A. Madhavan, Kashyapan, M. Dakshinamurti, Sharavana Subbho, Hephzibah Yesudasan – the second-generation writers – introduced modernism in Tamil literature; Thoppil Muhammed Meeran, Nanchil Nadar, Poneelan – the third generation of writers; and myself, Kumaraselvi and H.G. Rasool, who belong to the fourth generation of writers, have all actively contributed to it. In each period, at least one–third of the prominent writers from Tamil Nadu were natives of this land. After Thanjavur, this is the most familiar place to the people of Tamil Nadu because nothing captures the spirit of a place as beautifully as literary works. Any Tamilian who reads

Tamil literary works will definitely be familiar with Marthandam, Thenghapattinam or Kulachil.

Once a writer from Chennai said in a forum, 'The writers of Nanchinadu are indeed blessed. The geography of their land is one that the average Tamilian dreams of; their lifestyle is one that is unfamiliar. To be born in a land that retains its individuality is a blessing for any writer. Even if he merely writes about what he sees and hears, as literature it becomes exotic.' Piqued by the implied denigration, I answered, 'The writers of Nanchinadu are like the dog in Joseph Brodsky's famous poem who raises his leg to piss on the non-existent wall of the broken-down church. The life they write about no longer exists, save in their imagination. The strength of their writing is because they defy imagination with imagination.'

Recently, A.K. Perumal and I were passing through Azhikiya Pandiyapuram on his scooter. Below the wall of a huge, ruined stone house, we saw a tiny shop. Calling it a shop would be a mockery. There were just a few plastic jars of sweets, beedis and paan on an old deal box and some bananas. Behind the box, on a stool, sat a thin, old man, bent with age, white-haired, his empty stomach folded in. A small, young girl stood next to him, wearing a torn frock – his grandchild. A.K. Perumal said this was the present Mudaliar of Azhikiya Pandiyapuram!

3

Daughter, Mother, Woman

I

With You

Inside the room, the murmur of voices. Chaitanya is talking to her friends. When I went in and asked her, 'Where is my red shirt?', the voices went down a notch. Silently, she pointed a finger. I picked up the shirt and walked out. Behind me, someone closed the door soundlessly.

I sat down in the sitting room and mused. What would a little girl studying in the eighth standard have to discuss behind closed doors? I shouldn't think like that. Behind each person, another person's door is closing shut, softly; like closing eyelids, softly; like lips after conversation, softly; like curtains after a performance … it is closing.

Yet, this is my daughter. I saw her first when she was still inside Arunmozhi's womb, on the screen of the ultrasound machine – an image infused with life. She yawned tiredly on screen and turned her back to us. 'Nothing much to gain from coming out' – that seemed to be her attitude! Even when the full term was over, she stayed on for four or five days before making her appearance.

From the second day onwards, I was the one who bathed her. A tiny bundle of joy, a minuscule seed, a beautiful word a stranger had spoken in an unknown language. Her haemoglobin levels were low. So I placed her on my feet and sunned her. Those days, I was immersed in the Kamba Ramayanam. The tender rays of the sun fell on the thicket of words on the open page. I saw the blood redden in her tender ears, drunk on sunlight.

To witness a girl evolve is an amazing experience for any man. The baby who looks at you, smiles and turns over, is not merely your child, but also your mother. The moment her tiny arms straightened, she started kissing her doll, feeding it and rocking it to sleep. She carried the dolls wherever she went. Whenever she found a towel, she turned it into a cradle. The Tamilians believed that those born as our daughters were our mothers in our past lives. 'Weren't you my birth mother?' they coo to their daughters lovingly.

We only notice the passing of seasons when they leave us. The trees and birds know when spring will come. But we, who sing 'grow little hands, grow little feet' to our young ones, do we at some point start telling time, 'Go a little slow, you racehorse!'?

I wondered if I should go and quietly open the door. I desisted. I was afraid I would meet an unknown woman inside the room.

II

Sisters

The day Ajithan's exam got over, he asked my permission to go out with his friends to watch a movie and have a smashing time. Smashing was meant literally. Anything that could be broken in school would get broken that day. I said, 'Yes.' As the boy was leaving – looking like a young dude in his jeans and shirt, his hair slicked back – Arunmozhi said, 'Take her with you. She is bored sitting at home!'

'Get lost, Ma,' the boy retorted, 'as if I have nothing else to do! I can't.'

His mother did not understand why he was so upset. 'What is wrong if she comes with you? Isn't she your younger sister? Why can't you take her along?'

Ajithan was shaking with anger and frustration. 'Okay then, I'm not going anywhere.' He began taking off his shirt.

'This boy's arrogance is impossible. Come here and ask what is wrong with him.' Arunmozhi called me.

When I walked in, the boy was crying bitter tears. His sister stood nearby trying her best not to laugh.

I said, 'Leave it, Aruna, let him go. How can we allow her to go with him?'

She didn't get it. 'Why not? Isn't she his sister? Didn't he take her everywhere till now?'

I sent him on his way and sat her down to explain things to her. She merely said, 'You are imagining all this, he is still a child.'

True. Until now the girl had been his shadow, tailing him everywhere, thinking the same thoughts – an echo. If he said, 'My! How enormous!' she would respond with, 'My! How enormous! Show me, Aji, show me.' Yet a time comes when even the lizard gets rid of its own tail.

When I was young, Viji was my tail. I remember her when she was a baby. I have memories of her as a baby lying on a mat. Someone stooped to kiss her. I thought he was going to eat her. 'Don't eat the baby!' I screamed, breaking into tears. Everyone around me burst into laughter.

Many images follow that. She was a plump baby, her skin the colour of honey. When my mother gave her a bath, I would sit next to her, my hand on her tummy, feeling the warmth of the warm water flowing down. I would touch the black spot on her left cheek put there to protect her from the evil eye and add another on her right cheek to make her look doubly pretty. When they put her on the mat in the veranda, when the house rocked in the moving shadow of the coconut palm leaves, I'd gently rub the tender pink skin of the instep of her feet.

Viji was younger than me by a year and a half. When she was born, my father named her Lakshmikutti, after his mother. My uncle, his younger brother, changed it into Vijayalakshmi. In looks, she took after my father. When she was around fifteen, she went to the school in Kazhitura for a function there. Seeing her, one of the older teachers asked her, 'Are you Bahuleyan Pillai's daughter?' He had taught Father in school. The teacher had last seen him when he stalked off after his tenth exams calling out, 'Goodbye bastard'. Often, when someone saw him on the street, they would stop him and ask, 'Aren't you Lakshmikutti's son? We have a property case going with your mother.' In our home town, almost everyone was engaged in a civil case over property with Grandmother.

Generally, girls start speaking early, but Viji spoke in monosyllables till she was three. She expected – no, demanded – that people should understand her needs from her facial expressions and act accordingly. Mother used to go crazy. Viji would get up in the morning and start weeping silently. If you asked her what the problem was, there would be no response. 'Open your mouth and say something, you devil's spawn,' Mother would swear. Sometimes, in desperation, Mother would box her ear. Nothing. Mother would admit defeat and plead, 'Darling, I made a mistake and hit you, tell me what you want.' Nothing. Then she would turn to me. 'Ask her what she wants and let me know.' I was her tongue. I would say, 'The baby wants jaggery.'

She followed me everywhere like a quiet pet dog. If someone saw me on my own, they would tease me: 'What happened to your tail?' I talked to her incessantly. Words flowed from my mouth. Mother would ask in exasperation, 'What are you gibbering constantly, like a dog pawing at a palm leaf?' No one but Viji could understand what I was saying.

Those days I was a composite being of four or five people. One wanted to fashion a huge wing by stitching crows' wings together and fly in the sky. Another wanted to build a house on top of the palm tree. The third wanted to write a huge tome too big to lift. Viji was with each one of them. When I tried to teach a dog to speak Tamizh, she helped me and got bitten in the process. 'He is crazy, you are a girl, no? What happened to your brains?' Mother chastised her. She shed silent tears whenever someone scolded me.

Among his children, father preferred Viji. I don't remember him hugging me ever. If I had to climb somewhere and he had to lift me, he would hold me by the waist and hoist me up. I desperately longed for the touch of his hands, and when he touched me, I held on to that memory for years. For Father, my elder brother was a fellow human being with whom he could discuss his thoughts and inquire of him as to his whereabouts. Me, he just scolded once in a way.

As long as Viji was a child, every morning Father would call her close to him and cuddle her. As soon as he had had his tea, he would come to the front veranda, sit in the easy chair and call out, 'Girl.' Viji would reluctantly go forward, attitude dripping from her! Father would circle her waist with his hand and draw her close.

'How are things?' he would ask. That's all he knew to ask.

He would repeat it again and again. Viji would remain silent. Scattered, single words, a few squawks, that's all one could hear from them.

Two animals wordlessly loving each other.

From behind the window, I would watch the scene. My father did not like me watching him. So I'd hide in the room and peer through the window. 'Why can't this puppy open her mouth and say something?' I'd wonder. I had so many things to share with my father. If only he cooperated, there were so many projects I wanted to do with him.

My father knew I was around. If he had any sweetmeat to give to Viji, he would call out, 'Boy!' I'd appear immediately. 'Take it. Give it to her as well. Don't hog everything.' He knew very well what would happen. If I asked Viji she could not but give her share to me, and I could not help but ask.

I would ask her again and again what father had said to her. She didn't know how to answer him, and he wouldn't have said anything much either. Yet her silence infuriated me and I would slap her. She would weep silently. 'When I go flying in the sky, I will not take you,' I'd threaten her. She would start wailing. If anyone asked her what I had done to her to make her cry, she would remain resolutely mute. She never complained about me.

Once, I wounded her on her chest with a scrap of metal I had picked up from outside. I never expected to see so much blood. It was Onam day. Viji was sporting a beautiful new sky-blue nylex full skirt and blouse. I had the usual khaki trousers on. Father did not care for boys wearing colourful clothes or applying talcum powder on their faces. Why couldn't boys wear nylex skirts, I raged.

'Get lost, get lost,' I chased Viji away.

She stayed at my back, and I attacked Viji's. When I saw the blood, terrified, I ran to find Mother. 'Viji fell down and hurt herself,' I lied.

Mother came running. By that time, Viji's whole dress was soaked in blood. I embroidered my tale. 'As soon as she got up from her fall, she picked up a metal piece and cut herself.' Mother slapped me, hard. When I fell down, she grabbed the hard wooden stalk of a coconut leaf and started beating me. I managed to stop her the second time and ran away to hide in the bushes.

I decided that I would live like a wild beast, foraging for food, but I couldn't find anything to eat. When it grew dark, I began to feel frightened. I returned home to see that Father was back. The doctors had sewn up Viji's wound and had given her a tetanus shot.

'Come, let him decide what to do with you. Today you really crossed the line.' Amma took me to Father's side. Father was resting in the easy chair. She stood at the door behind him and said, 'The boy has come.'

'Umm,' Father grunted.

'He is becoming really wild.'

No response.

Mother waited patiently.

'Don't you want to ask him?'

He spoke: 'Let it go.'

Disappointed, Amma said to me, 'Go to sleep.'

I moved towards the kitchen. When I was a child, my father only beat me for insignificant things. For significant things, he was convinced that I would recognize their gravity on my own.

While I was eating my dinner, Viji came and stood next to me. She smelled strongly of iodine. 'Get lost!' I shooed her away. I had been eaten alive by fire ants because of her – fat, red, head-heavy ants. They bite you and fart a sour wind. Instead, Viji came closer and held out her hand, 'Do you want candy?' I looked. There were four or five red-coloured candies nesting in her palm. 'Do you have more?' I asked. 'I ate one. They are sweet. But at the very end they are bitter.' I began eating the candies.

Soon I turned into an avid reader. Viji didn't read. I would tell her stories from the novels I read. Those stories transformed into my stories. While at home, Viji had a habit of doing something all the time. She would be cleaning the tamarind or removing the spine from the coconut leaves or making mats outs of palm tree leaves. While she worked, I'd sit next to her and narrate stories of the heroes from the historical novels of Sandilyan (Bhashyam Iyengar). She would listen quietly, a small smile hovering on her lips. Later, those heroes transformed into the idealistic heroes of Jayakanthan's novels, into Sundara Ramaswamy's rebellious thinkers and into Kafka's baffled young men!

When my first short story came out in print, it was Viji I first shared it with. With the money I received for it I bought a brocade tassel for her hair. Was she following me in spirit even then? I spoke to her of Vivekananda, of Aravindan and of Ramanan. But later, without even my realizing it, I stopped talking to her.

Solitary, caught in an inner world, I drifted all alone. Now and then, when my feet took me home, she would come and sit beside me quietly. I'd looked at her from a long way away, from the summit of an insurmountable hill. She did not know what was beyond that hill. When I was in the final year of college, I ran away from home. I had no idea why I was going away or where I was going or for what. I just felt I had to go – like Kafka said, 'far from here'. That was all.

I returned after a month. A few days at Siddhavanandan's ashram, a few days at Tiruvannamalai ... More withdrawn and silent than before. Father was in the hospital after his first heart attack. When she saw me, my mother hugged me hard, like a deranged woman, and cried. My neighbour, Keshu uncle, said, 'We thought your elder brother would go mad. For a month he was roaming around all over the place looking for you.'

Viji only looked at me from a distance, a tear hovering beneath her gaze. When the intensity of emotions subsided, I became, once again, the forgotten one. One day, when I was sitting in the lean-to at my desk, Viji came to my side, her eyes heavy with unshed tears. I sat looking at her. She merely said, 'Brother, when you go next, please say one word to Mother.' Ten days later, I left home again. For a year and a half I wandered here and there, mostly in Kashi and the Himalayas. When Viji asked me to tell Mother before I left next time, I wasn't even thinking of leaving. But Viji sensed it. The only person who knew that I was about to leave was Viji.

III

Women

What is my first memory? After pondering for a long time, I had it fixed. The memory rose from the depths, unbidden, while I was in the throes of the raging fever I suffered when I was ten. Soft young feet. I am crawling, haven't yet started walking. I must have been around six months old. A small kitten. I am trying to balance a tiny basket made of palm leaves on its back. Someone laughs. The moving, bottom fringe of a saree blooms like a big flower. At the centre, like pistons, a pair of legs. The legs come close, hands reach out and lift me up. I kick my legs, trying to get down.

My second memory. I am sitting on the bank of a pond. The cement on the retaining wall has become pitted with age and rain. A cow looks at me and comes forward threateningly, as if to gore me. I can easily fit between its horns. I am so tiny. I cannot cry out – I am frozen with fear. Suddenly a pair of cold, wet hands reach out from the pond and pluck me to safety. As the lady presses me to her bosom, she keeps shouting at the cow to scare it away.

When I started learning meditation, this memory surfaced and grew in clarity till it became a vivid image. When I told my mother about it, she looked at me in shock. Apparently, this had happened when she visited her parental house in Nattalam. Convinced that her husband would react violently if he heard about it, she had never mentioned it. My clear description of the pond and the sounds of the people in and around it surprised Amma so much so that she kept repeating the story until the end of her life. What I didn't mention to her was my memory of Janaki aunty, the woman who plucked me to safety. I could clearly recall the sparkle of the water drops on her bare shoulders, the wind-blown tresses against her cheek and the pimples on her fair skin.

The consciousness of women as women was there inside me even when I was just a year old, probably even before that. Maybe I was born with this sense in me. I have never talked about it to anyone, lest they should think I am mad. Once when my mother and I were travelling by bus, a young woman who was sitting behind my mother took me from my mother's hip and placed me on her lap. I kept sliding down because she was wearing a soft, slinky saree. She showered kisses on me. I can still remember the smell of her clothes, the faint smell of her sweat, her lips, her neck with its dusting of talcum powder, the flash of the gold chain around it – I remember it all. Most of my memories from childhood feature women.

I think it was in Munchirai. Three families were sharing a house. I remember visiting a neighbour, and she was breastfeeding her baby. She pulled the baby's mouth from one breast and was in the process of shifting it to the other. She looked up and asked me something. I stood there looking at her white, round breasts. She didn't realize that I was mentally capturing an image that has stayed fresh in my mind even after forty-six years. I remember thinking then that they looked like big bronze vessels. When I look at old photographs of myself – a thin, emaciated boy with an oversized head and glinting eyes – I am convinced that 'this current I' was already within him.

I was around ten. There was a function going on in the neighbour's house. A number of women had arrived from the neighbouring villages. The women were busy making *murukku* and kheer. All day I hung around them. At night, two or three women came over to sleep in our house. Among them was a young woman – our neighbour Vijaya's friend. By then I had turned into a boy who was very shy. When women meet shy boys, they try to engage with them and watch them grow more shy. I merely looked at the young woman from the corner of my eye. She was wearing a yellow saree, the colour of amaltas flowers. At night, she removed her saree and hung it on the clothes line. She wore the dhoti that my mother handed her. All of them slept in the big bedroom. The windows were left open to let in the breeze. Even after the light was extinguished, the women whispered to each other for a long time. I slept, lulled by their whispering voices. When I woke up sometime in the night, there was an amaltas in full bloom over my head. It took me a moment to realize it was her saree. In the light of the petromax, the saree moved animatedly in the breeze. That amaltas-flower saree was my first woman.

IV

Lost

Twenty years have passed. I have almost forgotten the young man who was searching for a place to sleep at the Jhansi railway station in Madhya Pradesh. Those days, security wasn't this tight, and no one asked any questions. At the railway station, a homeless person could always find a place to sleep, away from the sun and rain. Railway stations attracted many wanderers – nomads like *Lambada*s and *Kurava*s, prostitutes, lunatics and stray thinkers.

The Jhansi railway station was huge. The city itself had not grown so big. It was the central point on the axis of the railway map of India. Trains that ran east–west and north–south converged at Jhansi. It was late afternoon when I walked into the railway station. Rusty iron junk lay wet and scattered. Dried shit, old, discarded clothes, polythene covers, the partial grin of a dead dog, the stink of urine drying in the sun.

I longed to rest my head. I had a raging fever. I had just arrived at Jhansi, ticketless and hungry from Nellore in Andhra Pradesh. I had pinned the last remaining ten-rupee note to the inside of my shirt. The sun was in my eye. A disused grain shed, long abandoned, lay before me – wall-less. On its floor wheat had sprouted and grown. The holes in the roof created crystal pillars of sunlight. No one was likely to disturb me here. In the right-hand corner was a toilet, its broken walls supported a variety of vegetation. I had to rush out gagging before I finished urinating because of the stink. People who used the shed to sleep probably used the toilet, too.

Behind the toilet the ground was covered with undergrowth. A few palm trees grew wild in it. I was looking for a place to sleep when I saw the girl – a dark, emaciated, ten-year-old. She was wearing an old, torn, red salwar-kameez. She had spread a cinema poster on the ground and was lying on her stomach on it, reading a book. Beside her sat a naked one-year-old playing in the sand. What surprised me was that she was reading! I had seen many children like her while I was wandering aimlessly across the length and breadth of India. They were all illiterate. The book the girl was reading turned out to be a small novel. She had finished more than fifty pages of it. The baby at her side looked at me and smiled. He had two milk teeth. Pushing back the strands that fell on her face, the girl lifted her face from the book, looked at me and asked, 'What?'

I shook my head, indicating nothing. I found a place a good distance from her that was sandy and dry. I took out a towel from my bag, spread it on the sand, placed the cotton satchel on it for a pillow and lay down. The girl got up, came to my side, looked at me and smiled. Standing there, I could see that she was severely undergrown.

'Do you speak Hindi?' she asked.

'No.'

'Madrasi?' she inquired, smiling.

I brought out the one word I had used extensively while travelling in north India.

'*Jao*, go.'

She put her forefinger in her mouth, sucked it and looked at me. 'What?' I asked, uncomprehending.

She repeated her actions and said, 'Five rupees.'

Blood rushed to my head. A shiver passed through my body.

'Go, go!' my voice quivered.

'Give money.' She smiled again. Between her dark, dry, thin lips, I could see dark gums and stained teeth.

'Go.' I turned my back to her and tried to sleep.

'Brother, give me one rupee.' I searched for a stone to threaten her with.

She laughed and moved away.

When I turned to look a while later, I could see her reading again. The child was grabbing fistfuls of sand and filling his lap with it. He looked at me, pointed to me with his hand and smiled.

Time passed. I noticed a man wearing a loose, white kurta-pyjama and a Gujarati cap talk to her – a middle-aged man with a prominent, bulbous nose. He didn't see me, and the girl did not point me out to him either.

Both disappeared inside the toilet. I couldn't bear to even look that way.

I got up. When I went up to the baby, he smiled at me and offered me a fistful of sand. I picked up the book and looked at its cover. It had the picture of a girl with bobbed hair holding a badminton racket. Down below was an image of a man's head. Something was written on it in letters that looked like clothes hanging from a clothes line. A colourful, cheap paperback.

I returned the book to its place and looked at the kid. He seemed accustomed to being on his own. He was smiling at me. I wanted to smile back but couldn't. I picked up my bag and started walking along the old, red, rusty rail tracks and crossed over to the main road on the other side of the tracks.

V

Broken Relics

Today my stories have an identity. It is an identity I have forged with a language that is my own – stories of yakshis, of elephants, of heroism and myths. I am not a modernist writer. I am a representative of the hoary literary tradition of South Travancore. Most of the modernist Tamizh and Malayalam writers will not last more than fifty years. I will be there forever. I am not a writer of prose; I am a poet – a poet who writes in prose. Seeking my stories and their origins, I have wandered far and wide. For my stories, I have visited old homesteads in remote, tiny villages in South Travancore. Much later, when I met the chronicler of South Travancore's history, Thrivikraman Thampi, I realized that I too had visited most of the places he had wandered to over his lifetime.

If you look at the great temples of South Travancore, the image they evoke is that of a great tusker slowly but inexorably sinking into a bog. This tusker has an impressive forehead, long tusks and a trunk. But it is an animal that belongs to the prehistoric era and, like the chariots cast out of molten metal, its solidity and strength are superfluous qualities today. What is needed today is agility – to live in the moment, to backtrack. The temples of South Travancore retained their glory as long as the king was on the throne. The decline of the temples started with the nationalization of temples by Colonel Munro, but their real deterioration began when India became independent.

The temples today look like the broken relics of an ancient, forgotten civilization. Broken tiles, loose masonry, cobwebbed dining halls, dark, sleepy, smoke-stained dance halls. Sacrificial stones, lost among wild thickets, and between them flow lonely paths. Inside one of these temples you will find a priest, bent with troubles, pale like the root of a coconut tree, who is paid just a few hundred rupees a month as salary. From the scent of the sandalwood paste that he drops in your hand, indifferently, you know that its time is past.

Beside the temples, on either side of the road, you can see old, large tiled-roof houses. Some of the tiles are broken or missing, and the once smoothly plastered walls are now pitted and scarred. Inside, only a few rooms are occupied; that too by old men and women with faces that have melted with the heat of time – wordless, like the statues inside the temple, with bewildered, uncomprehending eyes! Silence reigns, maybe because our ears are unable to hear their silent screams.

It was Potti from the temple who told me about the old lady who cleaned the premises. I found her house easily. A few steps led to a small gatehouse, inside which stood a few, tall, old, fruitless coconut trees. Beyond the yard stood a huge, ancient house. Its plaster was stained ochre and the upstairs windows gaped open with broken panes. No one appeared to live there. When I called a few times, an old lady stepped out and asked in a disinterested voice, 'Who is it?'

I introduced myself and told her that I worked for a newspaper and was from Trivandrum. She looked uncomprehending, but nevertheless asked me to sit down and went in. Two young kids peeped out from behind the door, the younger boy clinging to the torn skirt of his elder sister. Both looked dying, sick, with pale, bloodless lips and dry skin. I asked their grandmother if she knew southern folk songs.

'No,' she said shortly.

She refused to answer any questions I asked her. Her whole being screamed at me, 'Get lost.' After a while, I could hear someone approach. A woman who looked around thirty was approaching carrying an uruli covered with a plantain leaf. With her was a young man who was mentally disabled. He had tiny eyes and wore a constant smile. He looked to be around twenty-five. When he saw me, he looked startled.

'What?' he asked.

I rose and told them the reason for my visit. The only lie I uttered was that I belonged to a newspaper.

'No one here knows any songs or dance, you go.' The young woman vanished inside, and with her went the kids and the old lady. The young man came to me, touched me and said, 'Rice! Rice!' I asked him to leave, but he stayed where he was.

I longed to leave but in situations like this, I had trained myself not to show any resentment. I sat there. The young man asked me if I wanted rice and invited me inside.

He had a soul that loved everyone. I liked him. I took out a two-rupee note from my pocket and gave it to him. He accepted it, beaming with happiness, remarking, 'This is for Leela, this is for Leela!' Leela must be his sister.

Immediately, I understood the situation. They lived in abject poverty. The rice the young woman had brought in the uruli was the offering from the temple. That was the only thing they had. Once upon a time, when temples used to cook a hundred *marakkáls*[1] of rice, they would have received cooked rice in abundance. Now, the Tamil Nadu government would give all the gods only a hundred ounces of rice. The old lady and the children had been waiting for that rice. It was then that I could comprehend the expression on their faces when they saw the woman walk in with the vessel.

'Haven't you left?' the woman asked as she stepped out.

'I haven't finished. These are songs I'm collecting for the newspaper. I get money for each song. If you sing those songs for me, I'll write a voucher and pay you.' She looked unconvinced.

I opened my bag and showed her. 'I will pay immediately.' She thought for a moment and said, 'Okay, I'll ask Amma to sing for you.'

The old lady came and sat down. She appeared utterly uninterested. The children had gone out to play. Maybe their mother had shooed them away.

I took out my notebook, tore a page from it, wrote out a voucher, got her signature on it and handed her a two-rupee note. The old lady handed the note to her daughter and started to sing, reluctantly. Her voice quavered. The song was about Kalliyangatu Neeli. Her son, the disabled young man, came close and sat at her feet.

The other lady came and stood behind her mother, next to the door. That's when I really noticed her. She was very fair and had long tresses that reached down to her waist. Although she was unnaturally thin and pale and had dark circles under her eyes, she was beautiful and dignified. In my imagination, she became a queen who was thin and starved because she was in hiding.

For the next song, I gave the younger lady five rupees. She took it and retreated inside. As she went in, she summoned her brother with her eyes. The brother withdrew his eyes from his mother and followed her inside.

As she sang, the grandma began to enter into the spirit of the song. In the places where Kalliyangatu Neeli showed her real image, the *vishwarupa*, her voice grew really loud. I was recording the songs on a tape recorder. The lady returned with a bronze vessel full of tea, without milk. She must have made it with the tea dust and sugar that the boy just bought.

For the next song, she joined her mother. She began singing the lines forgotten by the old lady, and then sang the full song.

'You sing very well!' I remarked.

'Oh! These are songs I learnt in my childhood.' She appeared embarrassed.

She sang the next song on her own. Her voice was deep. Through her voice emerged Panchavan Kattu Yakshi. In the moon-drenched land, she strode like a flame, her body a blazing red, her long, swaying curly hair like whorls of dark smoke. Her body writhed as she danced!

The woman asked me my name and the place I was from, and what I did for a living. From the depths of her eyes a flicker of laughter emerged, like the midday sun reaching the depths of a deep well. Then she told me about herself. Her husband drinks. He is a cook. He went to Trivandrum in search of work eight months ago. There has been no news of him after that.

Dusk fell. I got up to leave.

'Aren't you going to the temple?' she asked.

'I went. Didn't go inside,' I replied.

'Ayyo, after coming this far, don't go away without visiting the temple. It is a beautiful temple. The temple has a number of beautiful carvings. You should visit.'

I hesitated.

'You can stay here tonight. Tomorrow, early morning, you can bathe, pray at the temple and leave.'

I thought it was a good idea. I got her signature and paid her thirty rupees for the stay. When she took the amount from me, her face grew red with embarrassment.

The boy came with me to the temple. On the way he paused to point out everything that he liked. He smiled constantly. He was captivated by anything that flew. When we returned after the darshan, we found the children studying. The whole place was deserted and silent. Far away you could see a couple of flickering lights from other houses. There was no electricity in that area. The lights were from kerosene lamps. On the porch, the grandmother sat reciting prayers. My bag was no longer on the porch wall.

The young lady stepped out and said, 'Krishna, show him the room upstairs.'

One of the steps on the wooden stairs was broken. Upstairs there were four rooms. They smelled of dust. In one of the rooms, on a cot, was my bag. The room, which had been freshly dusted and swept, smelled of dust and cobwebs.

While I sat there writing, the lady of the house came up to invite me for dinner. In one of the rooms she had placed two plantain leaves – one for me and one for Krishnan. Krishnan looked ecstatic. 'Come, come, sit. There's rice … rice,' he said. She served rice, a curry made with ground coconut and a side-dish made with drumstick leaves. I had skipped lunch and was hungry. I found the food delicious. What astonished me was the speed with which Krishnan ate. When I turned our eyes met, and she smiled.

After dinner, I had hoped to talk to the grandmother, but she went off to sleep. All of them had trained themselves to sleep early to save kerosene. I went up to my room. The roof tiles in my room were broken in many places and I could see the stars through the gaps. I could hear the bats in the adjacent rooms. In the darkness I could hear the sound of someone moving; windows creaked and the palm leaves shuddered – like boiling sugarcane juice that thickens and goes on – till the night deepened and they fell silent.

When I heard the yakshi stories in bright daylight, they were just stories, but now, in the dark, they became real – yakshis who could see through their nipples, Neeli, whose lips dripped blood. When I closed my eyes, they acquired substance. Mentally, I jumped at the slightest sound. My being appeared to be standing guard for something infinitesimally tiny. What was it? Why was it that everything I had to remember became like this? It was like stirring salt into a sea of milk. When I finally slept, I was walking, freezing, in a valley of fear – an empty valley filled with imprints of lost, forgotten feet. The fallen flowers turn into eyes, the net-like shadows stir; far away a star shines, all knowing.

I wake up. I sense someone standing beyond the door. A shiver passes over me, like a wind through the waters of a lake. I gather my thoughts and in that awareness I realize that it was merely fear. I felt someone touching the door and the door quavering like the hide of a cow. I waited for a thousand years … ten thousand years. Buddhas after Buddhas, through penance became enlightened and rose up. As dew drops that swell and fall, moments flash silently and disappear.

Then I hear a faint call – 'Sir?' It is not a figment of my imagination. A knock on the door and a very soft call, 'Sir'! I become aware of the seconds that pass. I freeze into an ice-cold statue. It seems to last an eternity – in front of me civilizations rise and set. A sneeze comes up inside me. I stir. The person on the other side of the door stops knocking and says urgently, 'Sir, open the door.' Silence. In my imagination, I see her feet going down the stairs in the darkness. I watch myself silently writhing in agony and pain.

After that I cannot sleep. Thoughts tumble in my head. Sometimes I stop following the threads of thought and just sit, bewildered. Then the thoughts slip away, only to grow once again. I hear a cock crow, but after that I must have slept briefly.

I woke up at dawn and came down with my bag. Krishnan was sweeping the yard. His face brightened when he saw me. He said, 'I already had my tea.'

I walked up to the well and washed my face. For a moment I wondered whether I should just leave the place or walk back to the porch. The young woman stepped out and smiled at me, as though nothing had happened, and said, 'You have washed your face? I will bring tea.' In the bronze vessel she held out there was tea with milk. I couldn't look her in the eye.

She said in an ordinary voice. 'I came to ask you for a couple of hundred rupees.'

I raised my eyes, looked at her and hung my head.

'We are starving. On most days there isn't any rice in the temple. My children survive on drumstick leaves and banana stem.' Her voice cracked. 'This land and house are mortgaged. There's nothing here to sell.'

I put my hand in my pocket. Keeping aside the return fare, I gave her all the money I had with me. I walked out, my head hanging. I felt as though someone was chasing me. My body was soaked in sweat.

Many a time, I have wondered how embarrassed she must have felt to accept that money from me. I should have said something to alleviate her self-loathing. I should have told her how much I admired her. In reality,

I had only admiration for her. But I couldn't say anything. If I had opened my mouth, she would have turned into a yakshi. She would have burned and raged at any attempt at explanation. Good that I at least had the sense to keep quiet. After all, all the anger that Kalliyangatu Neeli felt was aimed at people who passed by.

VI

A Proposition

There was a time when people thought of me as a budding philosopher and Hindu seer because in those days I had a long beard, looked depressed and read the Gita. I sighed; I stroked my beard thoughtfully, my eyes fixed on the sky. If writing had not taken me over, I would have probably travelled a long way on that path.

Once, I, along with a sanyasi, went to see a well-known industrialist in Chennai. He was involved in many things – businesses, social service, revival of Carnatic music, breeding racehorses, etc. His mansion was huge and looked like a museum. Even the outhouse was as huge as a bungalow. It was there that I first saw the Great Dane. The industrialist had three of those dogs – two males and one female. In the night they roamed around the compound like lions, breathing loudly. During the day they had a room with air coolers to sleep in. They also had three men to look after them.

Technically, the industrialist's family lived there. In reality, they were scattered all over the globe. For people who came to visit these family members, there were five separate paths to the house, which had five sitting rooms and five garages! The outhouse at the back was air-conditioned. It had sofas and a TV.

The sanyasi who came with me was not interested in any of this. He was absorbed in writing a book. He wanted to create a comprehensive index for Vivekananda's thoughts in alphabetical order. He was in the process of rechecking whether the Swami had mentioned the same thoughts in different words. He had a habit of writing the same thing again and again, in different words. When he felt his hands ache, he would close his eyes and meditate.

Because I had nothing to do, I spent the days and nights sitting on the sofa and watching TV. Those days, TV in Chennai mostly showed Hindi serials. Watching them, I learnt words like '*shunya, shunya, shunya*'. Our appointment with the industrialist kept getting postponed. Once, when we met him briefly, he elucidated on *advaita* with the confidence that one generally associates with senior sanyasis. We couldn't present what we had come for, so we stayed on.

There were around fifty people working in that compound. Most of them did not have much to do. All of them were happy. The security men at the gate slept a lot. The manager was a man called Mani Iyer. His face, expressions, thoughts and language were those I had only seen among the Brahmins of Mylapore in Chennai. He was a great devotee. The walls of his room were filled with images of gods – standing, sitting, smiling and blessing. The pride of place was occupied by his favourite god, Dhanalakshmi, showering gold coins from both palms.

For some reason, everyone was respectful to me. None of the inhabitants took me for granted or spoke to me freely. When I stepped out the servants came and stood, arms crossed, waiting for me to tell them what I wanted. When I said 'Nothing', they withdrew silently. I walked around the whole bungalow. All the things inside were imported goods – expensive sofas, curtains, lamps, bed sheets – everything. The thought that it was an uninhabited museum strengthened in my mind.

Once, when I was sitting on the sofa, a servant came and deposited a few magazines on the teapoy in front of me. I picked them up – *Mangalam, Manorama, Saghi* and *Manorajyam*! Who read these Malayalam magazines there? As I was going through them, I heard footsteps on the stairs. A voice called a servant, 'Muruga, Muruga!' It sounded like a Malayalee woman. She came down the stairs. She was more beautiful than any woman I had ever seen before. At a glance one could make out that she was a Christian girl from Pala, the Changanacherry part of Kerala. She was exquisite. Her eyes, nose, lips, eyebrows – everything was perfect, as though drawn by a master painter. Not even a single blemish! It was difficult to pluck one's eyes away from her face. I stared at her open-mouthed! She came down and looked at me. She appeared surprised to see me reading the magazines. I gave her the magazines. She smiled and said, 'Thanks.' My brain kept repeating a phrase over and over, 'How beautiful!'

I desired to know more about her but could not bring myself to ask her directly. However, the next day, while I was strolling in the garden, she gestured to me, inviting me upstairs. I went up.

'Are you a Malayalee?' she asked.

'Yes,' I affirmed.

'What's your name?'

I replied. Her name was Alice. She was indeed from Pala. She was working there as a home nurse.

'For whom?' I asked, surprised.

'For the boss. He has sugar, BP and other issues.'

I couldn't understand. She stayed there all alone. The industrialist returned quite late at night and left early in the morning. How could she look after him?

'Do you stay here, upstairs?' I asked.

'Yes. I have my own room here. I never go down.'

I felt she was like a princess in a fairy tale, shut in an enchanted world. A strange life indeed!

I went with her into her room. It was a different world. The curtains, sofas, walls – everything was in shades of green.

'Sir likes green colour,' she explained.

'Do you live here?' I asked in wonder.

'Yes.'

'Alone?'

'At night, sir will be there.' Her eyes dimmed. I refused the bait and remained silent.

Her room was really messy. Worn clothes lay strewn on the bed. On the floor, an underskirt lay where she must have stepped out of it. Magazines were scattered all over. Even the surface of the mirror was covered with used sticker-bindis.

She asked me about myself. She was shocked. She couldn't believe that both my parents had killed themselves.

'Really? What was the trouble between them?'

She couldn't comprehend the issue when I tried to explain it to her.

'Who will kill themselves for something like this?' she wondered.

'There's no big reason behind birth. It's better not to have a big reason for death either!' I smiled. It was these kinds of responses that cemented my reputation as a philosopher. But she couldn't understand what I meant.

When I told her I was working for the telephones and I was posted in Kasaragod, she asked, 'Will you get leave?'

'There's nothing like that. I am a temporary employee.'

I wanted to know more about her. I asked her why she confined herself to the first floor. 'Almost all the people downstairs are Brahmins, and they hate me. I eat fish, no? The security brings me the fish from outside.'

'Do you visit your native place?'

'I go for Christmas, or if there is a wedding or some such function in the family.'

'Who is there at home?'

'My mother and my three younger sisters. My father died when I was very young.'

The picture was becoming clearer.

'What did you study?'

She hesitated. 'I passed the pre-university.'

'You haven't studied nursing?'

'No. I have a three-month diploma in nursing.'

After this conversation I tried to avoid her completely, but I could sense her eyes following me everywhere. After four days, when I returned to my room, I was shocked to see her talking to my friend, the sanyasi.

I didn't say anything.

'What happened? Are you ill?' she asked.

'No,' I replied shortly.

'I thought you had fever. Over here there are too many mosquitoes and fevers are quite common.'

'I was busy reading something.' I sat down.

Maybe because she lived alone upstairs, she chatted all the time. I have only seen sixteen-year-olds talk like that. As she talked, an animated, innocent girl emerged from within. It was enchanting to watch her – her clear, bell-sounding laughter, the way she moved her head and her hands, the way her eyes looked up as she thought about something, the way she jumped up when she remembered something – everything was captivating! Women only talk like that when the male gaze is upon them.

Those days, Shankar was the most popular hero in Malayalam cinema, and he was Alice's favourite. 'It's charming to see Shankar blush,' she often repeated. Most of her conversations revolved around Malayalam cinema, but she had seen very few movies. There was cinema only when she visited her home town. Here there were only film magazines.

'Cinema is my life!' she proclaimed.

The serialized novels in the Malayalam magazines were cinema for her. 'I read, imagining Shankar as the hero.'

Those days, *Mathrubhumi* was serializing Ashapurna Devi's *Prothom Protishruti*. 'It's a different kind of novel,' she explained. 'I like those kinds too. In it, the girl becomes the fourth wife of a geriatric old man and goes to live in a huge mansion. She is treated as nothing more than a servant. I read it and shed tears.'

The next day she invited me to her quarters. I refused to go. 'You come to our room,' I said.

'Why?' She asked.

'The swami is there. No one will misunderstand us.'

Her eyes darkened. 'And if anyone asks, you can always claim that I came to you. Isn't it?' I immediately realized that she was not stupid.

'It's not that,' I said lamely.

'You can say that. I don't mind.'

The attraction she exerted over me frightened me. The way she looked at something, her laughter, her body, the sound of her voice – everything was flawlessly beautiful. The beauty of the yakshis! From the bottom of my heart, I desired to find some flaw in her. When I sat in front of her, I could think of nothing else but her flawless form.

Between us, boundaries melted. As she laughed, she touched me. As we climbed the steps, she held on to my shoulder. She started calling me 'Jeyan'.

Once, when I pulled a window open, my hand brushed against her breast.

I turned pale. 'Sorry.' She moved her eyes away with a smile on her lips.

I was shaking uncontrollably.

After this incident, I avoided her completely. I saw her searching for me but managed to evade her for four days. On the fifth day, she walked into our room. I was busy writing something.

She looked altered. Her eyelids were swollen, her eyes red-rimmed and her hair uncombed and uncared for!

She sat in front of me and looked at me intently.

'What?' I asked.

'Nothing.'

'Do you have fever?'

'No.'

My hand still sensed the feel of her breast. I avoided looking into her eyes.

'Can I ask you something?' she asked suddenly.

'Sure,' I replied. My heart was beating loudly.

She swallowed and said very softly, 'Why do you avoid me?'

'I don't. You just think that.'

'No. You are avoiding me. I know.'

I remained silent.

'Don't you like me?'

'It's not that I don't like you,' I croaked.

'Then?'

My eyes were fixed on the notebook.

'Can you marry me?'

I was not even sure I heard the question. My dry lips stuck together.

'You can't, can you?'

I couldn't open my mouth – words welled up and suffocated me.

'Why? Is it because I am soiled?' Her voice was angry.

I still remember that moment. I can extend that one moment into a year, into a lifetime.

'Yes,' I replied.

For a moment she sat still, her hand pressed on her chest, then she got up and ran out. As she left, her shoulder banged against the door. The door kept swinging for a long time after she disappeared.

I sat there distressed. It was the acute distress of a man condemned to hang the next day.

I stayed there for four more days. I went to see her a thousand times and asked her forgiveness. I hugged her hard and kissed her ten thousand times. It was much later that I realized that in this world, unspoken apologies and ungiven kisses far exceed the power of spoken apologies and actual kisses.

As I bid goodbye to that place, my body trembled. I felt her watching me as I left. My stomach was knotted in tension.

After a month, when I was back in Kasaragod, I received a phone call from Madras. I never expected it to be her. The moment I heard her voice, I ceased to exist. I became one giant ear.

'Hello.' My voice was soft.

'Angry?' she asked in Tamizh.

'No! Why should I be angry? You are the one who should be angry.'

'*Ayyo*, no! I was the one who behaved cheaply. We knew each other only for eight days when I asked you. Later, when I thought about it, I was so embarrassed. I'm sorry.'

'Not at all. I was the one who said foolish things,' I tried to explain.

'I'm sorry. I called because I wanted to tell you that. Please don't think I'm cheap. That's all I want from you.'

'Honestly, I never think of you like that, I promise.' I was on the verge of tears.

'I shouldn't even have thought of such things. I realized that later. But at that point, it was quite a blow. I cried a lot. Now I'm all right. That's why I called.'

I wanted to tell her a hundred things. Cold, dead words inside me suffocated me. I couldn't utter a word.

'I want to say something with certainty. I did not ask you because I thought you were cheap. I've only respect for you.' She paused for a moment. 'People like me should not dream of things like that. I realize that. There are quite a few people like me here. They save money, and once their family is secure they go back home, marry someone and live happily. Somehow, I can't do that. I cannot lie and cheat someone.'

I found my voice. 'True, telling lies is wrong. But the problems that arise when you tell the truth will be much bigger than the problems that will arise if you keep quiet.'

She was silent for a long moment.

'Christ! I never expected Jeyan to say this to me. Christ! How can I hide such a sin ... ?'

'The question is not of purity or sin. If you don't mention it, it does not exist. You can make it vanish just like that.'

'How?' She sighed.

'Through love,' I said.

She sighed again and said, 'That will not happen.'

'It will happen. Wait and see.'

She was silent for a long time and then asked, 'What's wrong with telling the truth?'

'A man who wants you in spite of knowing this will be attracted only by your outer beauty. You will not like such a man.'

'Christ! It's true!' she cried. 'Let me cut the call. I'll never call again.'

Twenty-two years have passed. Maybe she has grown-up kids, or maybe she is a spinster. I don't know. What I know is that I hadn't shared anything significant in my life with her. This was the most important thing for me. This is how I responded. The rest of it, the narrative, was created by the brain. When she asked 'Is it because I'm soiled?', I didn't think before answering 'yes'. It was completely me. I didn't know the answer, and the answer I gave her was completely accidental, as unexpected as a number resulting from a throw of dice. I didn't know if it would be a six or a zero. It was as unexpected as finding Arunmozhi six years later.

VII

Finding Love

We got married on 8 August 1991. I was twenty-nine while Arunmozhi was barely twenty. A year before, in December 1990, I had published my first book. It won the Akilan Memorial prize. With it I started getting recognition as a writer. A number of meetings were organized in different cities to facilitate critical discussion on the book. In one such meeting, which was held in Coimbatore, a wit remarked that there was a matrimonial advertisement on the back cover of the volume. Everyone roared with laughter. While returning on the train I looked at the book once again. It was true. It read like a matrimonial advertisement. The publisher Kannan of Tamizhputtakalayam, who published the novel, had asked me at the last minute to send him a bio note. I didn't know for what, but I sent him one and he put it on the back cover of the book. I looked at the 'advertisement' and smiled. The old woman sitting opposite looked at me suspiciously. I am the bright one who advertises for marriage on the back of a book – a thousand copies of which will be sold over a five-year period! But that day, when I reached my office, the first response to my 'advertisement' was lying there on my desk – a letter from Arunmozhi.

Arunmozhi was a student at the Madurai Agricultural College. The letter was written by her and her friends. They had bought my book *Rubber*, had read it and were writing to me to convey their rage. 'What sort of novel is this modernist novel? Is this meant to be understood only by the writer? What is wrong if you can make it comprehensible for the reader? We read *Rubber*. It's fractured. There is no continuity. Time itself is mixed up. One episode happens before India won independence, the next while the strike is going on? Are you mocking us?'

I wrote a reply and posted it. I looked at the handwriting in the letter I had received. It appeared like the handwriting of a high school kid. It was the name that attracted me – Arunmozhi Nangai. It was the Tamizh word for Subhashini. There are Tamizh versions of each name for the goddess. I looked at the letter and smiled. I remembered what the wit had said in Coimbatore. I can hardly believe it now, but then and there I decided to marry that girl!

When I received a reply to the letter, I set out for Madurai. By then my mind had conjured an image of her. She had wide eyes, like Thi. Janakiraman, she talked rapidly … my mind kept on creating and recreating images of her. Those days I was living in Dharmapuri, in North Tamil Nadu. It was a ten-hour journey to Madurai. During the entire journey to Madurai, my mind was actively engaged in imagining what Arunmozhi would look like.

I went to her college to see her. It was 11 January 1991. The agricultural college campus was like a large garden. We walked below the trees in full bloom. The road was carpeted with fallen blossoms. She was indeed the girl my mind had conjured – a girl from Thanjavur, the land of Thi. Janakiraman and the Cauvery!

I had travelled a long way to reach her. I longed to tell her the story of my journey.

In 1984, I was at the Mookambika temple. I was alone, a beggar. Suddenly, I felt an intense desire to go and see my distant cousin who was working as a clerk in the army. He was posted in Kannur, Kerala. He made me stay there and offered to find me a job. He wrote home and got my certificates and applied for a job on my behalf at the Kasaragod Telephone Department. I got the job. I stayed in a commune for comrades of Kasaragod Telephones.

In my heart, I was still a nomad who sought solitude. I worked only when I had absolutely no money left. It was a temporary job, fetching me two and a half rupees for an hour's work. After a while, I got sick of the comrades and they got sick of my silence. I rented a rundown house on the beach on the way to Kumbla in Mogral Puthur and moved there. It was owned by a Muslim family. I filled the entire house with books. I ate only when I was really hungry. I also wrote stories occasionally. While I was living there, I became acquainted with Sundara Ramaswamy, and through him Attoor Ravi Varma. They became my teachers, and together they made me a writer. I wandered between the shores of writing and madness. Twice I tried to kill myself. Days passed in a flash between long, sleepless nights.

One day, when I woke up, I felt dizzy. The whole world, everything I could see, had transformed into a rippling, watery image. In the afternoon, I went to see an eye specialist. He told me that my eyes had been affected by paralysis. He asked me a host of questions.

'Do you have a pinprick pain in your arms and legs?'

'Do you hear sudden sounds?'

'Does your body suddenly experience shock for no reason?'

Then he said: 'You have a severe nerve disorder. It is indeed paralysis, but as of now it is very minor. The eye has six muscles which enable it to move. Among them one, probably two, have been affected. So your left eye is unable to move, and you are now seeing two images instead of one.'

'Look,' he said, and held up his finger.

I realized that what he said was true. It was like watching a 3D movie without the 3D glasses.

The doctor covered my right eye with a bandage. 'Let the left eye move. It's good for you.'

I immediately phoned Attoor and informed him. I had absolutely no money with me. Attoor's wife, Srideviamma, took the receiver from him and ordered me to come to Thrissur immediately. I borrowed some money for the journey and set out. In the misty rain that was falling incessantly, Attoor stood with an umbrella at the railway station to receive me.

I consulted Dr K.G. Nair at Thrissur Medical College. After examining me and listening to my story, he remarked, 'You have really abused your body. You can be a wayfarer, but only a yogi can be a perpetual wayfarer. Your mind is in a state of high agitation. Because of that you should have taken extreme care of your body.

'When it comes to sleep, you really crossed the line. Without sleep there is no imagination, no art. Nowhere in the world will you see an artist who doesn't like to sleep. Your issue can be resolved in a fortnight, but it will recur. Only you can prevent that.'

Those days, Bharat Gopi, the Malayalam film actor, was also afflicted with partial paralysis, the same disease that affected me. The doctor said, 'He is an emotional man – an artiste. If people like him stay intentionally sleepless and go about their business, their body will be unable to take it. In reality, we know very little about this organ – our brain. We can only entreat it and wait patiently for it to respond.'

I stayed at Attoor's house for fifteen days. I recovered within ten days. While I was staying there, Attoor broached the topic of my marriage.

'Sanyas is not for writers. That's for people who have steely resolve and tolerance.' Attoor and his wife suggested a few possible alliances for marriage. I couldn't commit to anything.

I courted Arunmozhi for only seven months. On the very first day I saw her, and as soon as I returned, I wrote her a ten-page letter clarifying my intentions. I had already told her about my life, its history and my future plans.

'At present I have a job that pays very little. One can barely survive on that. And I will never try to get a better job. Writing is my life, and through writing you will never achieve fame or wealth. I doubt if more than five hundred people will ever read my work. In fact, one can say that I'm actively striving for "failure" in life. But this is my dharma. If you can like all this, join me.'

Those days, I thought no girl would respond to such a letter. Now I think differently. I think any girl would respond to such a letter. There are very few girls who will be able to counter a man who is really determined, in a mad hurry. Arunmozhi wrote a reply but phoned me before I received it.

'I like you. I am willing.' And she burst into tears.

The same night I returned to Madurai. When I saw her in the morning my mind kept repeating the mantra, 'This is the one, this is the one!' By that afternoon we felt as close as a couple who had lived their entire life together.

We got married in a hurry. My love was like madness. I wrote to her every day; sometimes twice. Today, when I read those letters, I think my brain was not involved in their composition. But my heart was. Many people have observed that, in the last hundred years, I have been the one who writes the most beautiful Tamizh, but my most exquisite expressions can be found in these letters, which hardly anyone has read.

After she completed her course, Arunmozhi returned home. She took those letters with her and used to reread them. When her younger brother discovered her secret, she immediately left for Dharmapuri. We were married the next day.

My trade union friends were the ones who arranged everything. Everyone was enthusiastic. It was as though we had pulled off a minor revolution. In her borrowed silk saree and ornaments, Arunmozhi was trembling with a host of suppressed emotions. After the marriage we set out for Thrissur. As soon as we were alone, Arunmozhi began to cry.

'I'm thinking of my father. I can't forget his face,' she sobbed.

I was silent for a long time. 'Then why did you come?'

She wept.

After a long time she said, 'I decided that from now on, there will be only one person for me.'

Fourteen years later, some of the same friends who arranged my marriage and a few other friends got together with me for a literary event. By then, all of them were married. One had had a love marriage, the others had married women selected by their families. All of them had built houses, had children. A lot of water had flown under the bridge. We started talking about married life. There were around ten people in the room. None of them felt very positive about marriage. It was difficult to live without one – that was all. Every one of them had had disappointments, bruises, and a few beautiful moments. They all insisted that marriage was for the sake of children. The passion disappeared after a year. If you were able to have a child within two years, you were saved.

I sat silently. My relationship with Arunmozhi was definitely not like that. In all that time, we had never quarrelled. Nothing had happened between us to cause us mental agony or a misunderstanding. My passions, my thoughts – she shared them all. I had turned into a man who did not have any unshared thoughts!

My friends called Arunmozhi *rishipatni*, wife of an ascetic. But in that situation, amongst my old friends, I was not sure if I should talk about our relationship. Before my marriage, if someone had told me that their relationship with their wife was like mine with Arunmozhi, I wouldn't have believed them. I was convinced that it was human nature to only observe fellow human beings from a distance. I used to argue that it was impossible for man to keep aside his ego and be completely vulnerable in front of another human being. I was more a student of Sartre than of life.

As the night progressed, I became candid. In these fourteen years, my love for my wife had grown exponentially, I said. I retained the same longing and intense passion for her that I experienced as a young man newly in love. Even today, when I look at her, I said, I am filled with the same intense admiration that I had for her when we first came to know each other. Her movements, her expressions – they were the height of beauty for me. To me, no woman in the world was as beautiful as she, and I searched for her face in every face I saw. In fact, I felt that the feelings I had for her fourteen years ago were as nothing in comparison to what I felt for her now.

I thought the people in the room would mock me. But they grew silent. I said, almost challengingly, 'Yes, if a character in a novel said this, I would dismiss it as pure imagination. Maybe even now, if someone else said this, I would probably not believe him.'

What I said was the truth, and I know that from the core of my being. Every atom of my love sang to her. For me, everything, the whole world, was encapsulated in her. This was absolute *atmasamarpan* – giving of the self – the ideal that humanity has dreamed of for ten thousand years, what poets sang of, the theme of epics. This was that – nothing less.

Surprisingly, nobody laughed.

Only one person said softly, 'May I ask you something?'

I nodded.

My friend asked, 'Have you ever had intercourse with anybody apart from your wife?'

'No.'

'You have had chances?'

'Yes. I have always been noticed. There are very few writers of my generation who receive as much adulation as I do. So there were lots of opportunities. There still are.'

'Do you have a subconscious hidden from your wife?' he persisted.

I was confident. 'No. In fact, I doubt if I have a subconscious hidden from my readers. I believe that it should be so.'

'My last question: is your wife more important to you than your children?'

I paused. I knew how much my children meant to me. I said, 'Yes, my children mean a great deal to me, but Arunmozhi is beyond all that.'

Another friend who had remained silent so far asked, 'You are a disciple of Nitya Chaitanya Yati. Isn't the tradition to give oneself totally – *atmasamarpan* – to the guru?'

'Yes. But I couldn't, and Nitya knows that. I have told this to Nitya. He guffawed and said, "There's *advaita* in love. Sweet non-dualism." This is what Ashan the poet wrote about.'

For a while everyone was silent.

Then a voice spoke, 'You know, actually nothing that you said today came as a surprise to us. We knew this before you spoke. Today you put it into words. Till then you said the same thing through your actions. You have never spoken a thing without mentioning Arunmozhi. Why, you have never even given a public talk where you don't invoke her name!'

I was the one who was surprised then.

When we stepped out to drink tea at dawn, someone said, 'You are lucky. The energy behind your thought, its vitality, is love. Tolstoy mentions it in *War and Peace*. It's a rare occurrence – a coincidence. Or maybe there is something behind all this that we don't understand.'

As we were drinking tea, another person asked, 'Does your wife also have this intense love?'

'No,' I answered. 'It's impossible for her.' I felt a ripple of shock pass through the room.

'Arunmozhi is my best reader, my companion. Her love and respect for me are boundless. My world is her world as well, because from a very young age she has grown up with me. She is the editor of my works, the mother of my children.

'Boundless love is not for women. It is a blessing or a curse given only to men. However much a woman is in love, she doesn't give herself totally to it. Women have a measure, because they are also mothers. I have noticed this for a long time. In the beginning it used to bother me. I got the answer to my angst from the Kambha Ramayanam. There are many instances where Kambhan paints a vivid picture of the boundless love that Rama feels for Sita. But Sita's love is limited. Her love is not an adequate response to the great love that Rama feels for her because even before she becomes a mother, she is a mother. That's how Kamban portrays her.'

I continued, 'You should never expect women to experience all-consuming love. It is like expecting men to give birth. Any man who experiences intense love will die without ever receiving it in return with the same intensity. That is the rule of the game. After a point, a woman is only a mother. We can never hope to understand women fully. They are much greater than us.'

When Dr Manimegalai opened the doors and stepped out of the delivery room of her hospital in Dharmapuri and told me that it was a girl, I mentally touched her feet in gratitude. When she gave me permission to enter, I jumped inside and peered into the cradle. Chaitanya was sleeping, her lips parted, dreaming of a nourishing breast. A tiny red seed. 'It's a girl! A girl!' I happily proclaimed to the pale, tired Arunmozhi who was lying near her.

'So?' She was puzzled.

'She will be with me for many years. I can watch her take shape. It's like a tree growing in my cupped hands. Maybe I will be able to understand, after all.'

Arunmozhi just smiled a wry smile and closed her eyes.

4

Signs Left Behind by Ancestors

I

Matriarchs

At Thiruvattar, at my father's ancestral house, apart from the popular portrait of the Maharaja half turned and in his bejewelled crown, the only pictures that hung on the walls were of the two matriarchs. The elder one looks as though she were commanding the photographer to get it done with. She stands bare-shouldered, a gold-bordered dhoti tied tightly around her chest. The lobes of her ears are stretched in the fashion of the day, with heavy, traditional earrings. The other matriarch, her daughter, my father's mother, wears a jumper with a fine dhoti casually thrown over her shoulder. She looks into the camera, her head slightly tilted, scornfully dismissing the cameraman.

When she first visited the house, after walking along the length and breadth of it, exploring the rooms, the verandas, the courtyard, the kitchen and the attic, Arunmozhi asked, 'Why are there no photographs of the fathers?'

I had asked my grandmother the same question when she was alive.

Her response was, 'This is my house. Why should I keep their photographs?'

When grandmother went away into the house, her current consort, Kaipalli Gopalan, slammed the coconut he was dehusking on the digging bar, took off the towel he had tied around his head, wiped the sweat off his face, smiled broadly and said, 'Even if she wanted to keep them, she will need a photo gallery like the Pappanavaram[1] Palace, young one!'

She had many sambandhams.[2] Most of her partners were Brahmins.

When Arunmozhi repeated her question once again, I replied, 'I'm still searching. Once I find all of them, there is a possibility that I will compose an autobiography like Alex Hailey's. For Hailey, the issue was his roots. I don't have any issue with that. I am more concerned with the birds that lived in the tree for a brief while. The novel will be called *Birds*. What do you think of the name? Jokes aside, I have every intention to write an epic about my lineage.[3] Eight years ago, I even announced its name – *Ashokavanam*. In fact there has been a lot of discussion among the Tamizh literati about this unwritten novel! Meanwhile, I've finished three large novels. For some reason, *Ashokavanam* is yet to materialize. The matriarchs appear reluctant to talk in Tamizh. Now I have completely stopped trying to write it. Maybe one day it will come.'

Arunmozhi could not take her gaze away from the photographs. She said, 'They look like men.'

I was astonished. I knew grandmother when she was alive. She died at the ripe age of ninety, when I was in college. As far as I remembered, she was extremely beautiful. Her mother, my great-grandmother, too looked just like her.

'Why do you say that? Aren't they beautiful?'

Arunmozhi had difficulty explaining what she meant. 'Of course, they are beautiful. That's not what I meant. It's their demeanour. It's a man's demeanour.'

I couldn't comprehend what she meant. 'What demeanour?'

'If you hang my portrait along with theirs, how will it look?' she asked.

A light flashed in my mind. Arunmozhi would never hold her head in the manner they did. She would never look straight into the camera the way they did.

Her gaze and her manner would be tinged with shyness, like the touch of ruby on a green mango. I didn't know what to say.

'They are women, not *pathivrathas*. They don't owe allegiance to a single husband,' I remarked generally.

I talked about these matters extensively with her. In a photograph of Kavimani Desigavinayagam Pillai, he and his nephews are all seated on chairs. On the floor, smiling with her toothless gums, wearing *pambadam* earrings, sits his wife. There is a family photo of U.V. Swaminatha Iyer in his autobiography. His father is sitting on a bench, wearing rudraksha and holy ashes, holding a holy book in his hands. Below, on the ground, sits his aged wife, worshipping her husband with folded hands, almost like Hanuman in the image of Rama's coronation. In family photographs from Tamil Nadu, you can see long-dead women, their eyes dark with the pain of restless souls. It was this that impelled Subramania Bharathi to have a photograph taken of his wife sitting on a chair while he stood behind her. And if you look at Chellamma's face, you can be sure that as soon as the photograph was taken she would have burst into tears.

After her marriage, when my mother shyly stepped into the house for the first time, the marriage garland still fresh around her neck, this photograph must have greeted her – the photograph of her husband's grandmother looking at her, her dark, thick eyebrows curved upwards, unimpressed – the deathless look of scorn. If she was alive, I'd have asked Mother whether she was frightened. Her family is from Nattalam; their house is very close to the famous Shiva temple. My mother's father belonged to the Vellalar caste. Those days, among the Vellalars, those who followed the matrilineal system used to stay at the bride's house after their marriage. Padmakshi amma, my mother's mother, had eight children. Soon after the eighth child was born, she was afflicted with paralysis and was confined to bed. Her husband, the Vellalar, was pretty incompetent. Her cousin Dakshayani amma, the daughter of her aunt, came from Trivandrum to look after the kids. Padmakshi amma had asked her cousin, 'Elder sister, shall I die?' Her cousin answered, 'You die peacefully, my little one. I am there for your children.' Padmakshi amma died and Dakshayani amma brought up the eight children along with her own twelve – twenty children in all!

Nattalam is not Thiruvattar, where the river flows benignly. The land in Nattalam was elevated, the soil red. The only thing that could be cultivated there those days was cassava. Dakshayani amma brought up the kids on dried cassava and the plain white rice received from the temple. She died only after the eldest daughter got married and took over the responsibility of the family. In memory of the one who brought up ten kids per hand, the only thing that remained in that house was a huge cauldron. 'Mother used to fill this up with water and lift it all alone on to the stove,' my aunt reminisced.

My mother, growing up on dried cassava, stopped going to school after the third standard and started caring for her younger brother. She taught herself Malayalam and Tamizh and devoured novels in both languages. Along with her eldest brother, she too became a communist. The poverty of the family reduced after the eldest brother began to earn. It was only then that there was enough money for my mother to be married off. Among the aristocrats, the custom was not to marry off the daughters. The men arrived home to get married to the girls. But my father, an officer in government service, insisted that he wanted to bring his wife home. He didn't mind if the girl was born to a Vellalar father.

When my mother first stepped into her marital home holding a lighted lamp in her hand, her head bent as she was too shy to look up, her mother-in-law had exclaimed sharply, 'What are you searching for on the floor? Have you lost some money or gold? Walk with your head held high!'

My mother could never do that. When my short-tempered father shouted at her, she'd stand, dry-eyed, staring at him, and however much he thrashed her, she wouldn't take a single step back. She didn't know how to talk to people. She sat in the dark all night long, talking to herself.

Since there was hardly any money in my mother's family, the womenfolk in that family remained satisfied with just one husband. Around our house there were homesteads with extensive landed property. The women in those houses had multiple liaisons, multiple sambandhams. It was quite common for two husbands to coexist in one house. The children called them Elder Father and Younger Father. I realized that there was something odd about this practice only when the Tamizh boys in school teased me about it. The grandmother at Arapurakkal had two husbands, one to pursue the cases in court and the other to take care of the farmlands.

'Is the job of the other one to hold a lamp?' Chidambaranathan had asked.

I didn't understand what he meant. So I asked Mother. Mother said, 'Chidambaranathan is a very bad boy. You should not speak with him ever again.' She made me touch water and promise her that I would never talk to him.

As I grew up, I understood what he meant.

At first I was embarrassed. Later, through my study of anthropology, of cultural evolution, my understanding of it all evolved. Recently, when I spoke about this, I noticed that my companion, a man from Thanjavur, was growing visibly uneasy.

'In the two-thousand-year history of Tamizh poetry, only one thing stands on an equal footing in terms of the importance given to gods – prostitution.' Prostitutes were revered by the honorifics *parattai* and *urimai makalir*. They reveal to us that all men are captivated and capable of being seduced by women. Till recently, in an average village in Tamil Nadu, if there were a hundred houses, ten belonged to prostitutes. The wives who were abused and beaten up grew pale in dark, lightless rooms, or prostituted themselves secretly. While patriarchy reigned supreme in Tamil Nadu, women could only be slaves or prostitutes. Yet, in my culture there were no widows or prostitutes. To prove my point, I used the example of myths and legends from Tamil Nadu. If you considered the collection of ancient stories from Tamil Nadu, about half of them were about courtesans, while in Kottarathil Sankunni's *Aithihyamala*, there is not even one story about courtesans.

Arunmozhi couldn't get enough of my grandmother. Narrating to her story after story about her, my grandmother reincarnated in my thoughts. After her last husband died, my grandmother stayed without a man for thirty years. She single-handedly looked after her vast lands, the daily transactions and the challenges brought about by the changing social structure. She was a tall woman, very fair-skinned, and had a head full of white hair. Her hair was as white as a leghorn chicken. She even had a tiny bun at the nape of her neck that looked like the hen's tail.

When I see the Tamil actor Nassar, his nose reminds me of my grandmother's nose. She did not wear any jewellery. 'That is the custom of Tamil women. Ugly. How can well-born women walk around like chained buffaloes?' she would say.

She wore pure-white *vadassery* dhotis and a jumper with longish sleeves. Her walk reminded one of the villains who appear in the last scenes in a movie, striding forward, straight-backed, arms swinging, her mouth stuffed with paan, ready to thrash Nazir.[4] Her slippers were made by Karuvan Govindan. He cut strips from a used lorry tyre and attached to each a piece of leather to make her sandals. When she walked, she sounded like a buffalo moving. When she removed her chappals, they looked like two canoes.

Pure, landlordish behaviour! Before she asked you your name she would ask you your caste. She'd remember things in this order: first caste, then place, then any deformity or peculiar characteristic, then profession. The name was forgotten.

'That boy, the *thandan* from Kaliyal, that naughty boy, the one who taps rubber.'

'Ma, are you talking about Gopalan?'

'Yes. That boy. Once he told me …'

This was how conversation with her went.

She would ask the one-year-old son of Paraman Nadar of Mekkumalai, 'How are things, Nadar?'

When Potti's young grandson came visiting, she would jump to her feet and ask reverentially, 'When did your highness come?'

In our place, the people belonging to the barber caste used to be called *pandithar* since once upon a time they used to be *vaidyas*, Ayurvedic doctors, as well.

'That man, that *pandithan*, how can he alter the nature of his caste? If he was a well-born Nair, he wouldn't have kowtowed to China like this!' Grandma was expressing her anger at Pandit Jawaharlal Nehru's foreign policy.

Grandma was erudite. She knew Sanskrit very well. She rejected Sanskrit poetry and became enamoured by its grammar. She did not allow any man not well versed in Sanskrit to court her. She also knew English, but her knowledge was confined to understanding court documents in English.

Our landed property was a part of the lands over which the Nambudiris of Suchindram Vattapalli Madom had overall rights. Over the years, their expectation from the lands had dwindled. A couple of baskets of rice, four or five blocks of palm sugar and a sack of vegetables annually was all that was expected. One gifted these things and stood humbly before the Nambudiri and murmured, '*Adiyan* – my humble self', and the Nambudiri was satisfied. Those were the days when the matriarchs called all the shots.

Suddenly, out of the blue, our land was cut out from Travancore and made part of Tamil Nadu. The Nadar caste, who were farmers and tenants, organized themselves under their leader Neshamani and became powerful. Rajaji's cry, 'Land for the tiller', became law and made them landlords overnight. Grandmother could not comprehend what was happening. How could Kamaraj Nadar alter the laws of Shankaracharya and Padmanabha?[5] Nonsense! Grandmother took up cudgels against the Indian judicial system, and her co-conspirators were the old Fellow of Association of Law

(FA) advocates. She did not trust the advocates with the BL degree. She believed that if you were a lawyer, you slept wearing the advocate's white wing collars.

'You can be an advocate only if you wear a wing collar,' she insisted.

Grandma always carried a large leather satchel. It was stuffed with case files, land documents and various court case-related papers. She even folded normal pages lengthwise, like a case file. Why, she even folded her towels lengthwise! She had cases in the lower courts of Thakkalai, Kuzhithurai, Palliyadi and Parassala, and in the higher court at Nagercoil. To the best of my knowledge, she won only two of those cases but lost them too in the higher court. In the rest of the cases, when the judgments were delivered, Grandma would abuse the judges' lineage in Tamizh. Grandma swore and abused only in Tamizh. She felt that abuses in Malayalam lacked the necessary punch!

Later, she understood how things worked. Ownership of land was not decided by filing cases but by actual possession of it. She tried to wrest back her lands from the Nadars who had occupied them. Thugs came from Boothapandi and Kadukara, fattened themselves on eggs and chickens, exercised with wooden clubs and fought with the tenants. Apart from the civil cases, criminal cases also multiplied. Policemen wearing khaki knickers and putties, with oil-stained red caps, came calling. They discussed issues, burping in satisfaction after eating sumptuous meals, and left with their extended bellies and carrying gifts of plantains, coconut or palm sugar. One policeman asked for the cow tied in the barn and walked off with it. Once a month, Palliyadi Marakkar, the moneylender, came wearing his kerchief, attar and shampoo and took Grandma to the court in his horse-drawn carriage where she would sign parcels of her properties over to him. That day, we children would get new clothes and sweets. I was enamoured by the beauty of Marakkar's horse. Since it had a flower on its forehead, I assumed that it was a mare and named her Sundari, 'the beautiful one'. I was too young to know how to figure the sex of a horse.

There was nothing in common between Grandma and my father. He had left the house one night, soon after his matriculation. Inside the bedroom, his mother was sleeping with her latest husband. When he stepped across the threshold, with tear-filled eyes, he swore with his hands on his chest that he would never cross it ever again. He walked in the dark all the way to Nagercoil. Tired and hungry, he stopped at Thovala Kanji Madom to have some rice gruel and to rest. He started working in a tea shop at Valliyur. Later he moved to Madurai, where he tried his hand at various jobs. He acquired an impressive array of stinging abuses in pure Chentamizh, which he fell back on all his life when the need arose.

It was a time of change. The matriarchal system was on its last legs. Under that system, the rule of dividing property based on the people was advantageous to the women. Women, their children, and the grandchildren born to the daughters, all had an equal share in the property, while each son got only one share, and nothing for his progeny. Nair boys with scarcely any money went to Tamil Nadu to earn a living. That is how the tea shops, even today called Nair *kada*, came up throughout Tamil Nadu. My father too ran a tea shop in Madurai. Later he joined a ration shop as a salesman. He quickly got a job with the Tamil Nadu government. When he decided to assert his masculinity by bringing home a wife, he needed the help of his mother. The only time he had seen her in the intervening years was once in Kumarakovil. When she asked him, 'Aren't you Thankappan?' he pulled himself back. She looked carefully at the young man who had come along with the locals and sat down on the veranda. 'You have become a man,' she observed, and added. 'Your property is still here. I haven't sold it.'

In my memory, not once did my father look at his mother while talking to her.

Grandma lived all alone in her house at Thiruvattar. When the property was divided, she gave half her house to her children and lived in the other half. She had her own kitchen, cooked her own meals and ate all alone. Father built his own house at Thiruvarambu. His father, Shanku Ashan, was born in the Vayakka *veedu* family over there. He must have inherited a stick or a sword, because he wandered around fighting small battles and doing *marma chikitsa* – an Ayurvedic cure involving stimulation of vital points on the body. While thus drifting, he met Aarattil Lakshmikutti at Thiruvattar, fell in love with her and married her. The days of prosperity lasted only as long as his meagre stock of Sanskrit words lasted. One day, when he returned home, he found his areca-nut box outside, on the veranda.[6] He picked it up and held it to his chest, and crying piteously started walking from there. For two years he stayed at Thikkurissy. In one of the skirmishes he got involved in, he was kicked by a Tamizh wrestler and was badly injured. He stayed all alone in a lodge, in pain, his body bloated. After sixteen days he died. Someone must have cremated him. Vayakka *veedu* grew and split – into over a hundred families. The old homestead was near the Mahadeva temple at Thiruvarambu. It was mired in disputes and was left untouched for forty years. Then it slowly collapsed on itself. Around it grew trees and bushes. It was a large house, two-storeyed with an attic, its roof thatched with woven palm leaves (those days even the Padmanabhapuram Palace had a thatched roof). White ants ate away at the woodwork. Hoping to find buried treasure, the locals dug up its foundation. The walls of the house had keeled to the east. A big gatehouse and the compound wall were all that remained undamaged. The compound wall was a marvel. As fat as the stomach of an elephant, it stood tall at over ten feet. Made entirely of clay, it was smoothened with lime plaster, over which was applied a fine coat of putty. Even though the coating had broken off in some places, there was enough wall space for the locals to write abuses and carve symbols and messages on it. Leaving aside the ten and a half cents that was under litigation, my father bought the remaining one and a half acres at an inflated rate from a distant relative. He built a house there and named it Vayakka *veedu*. The old house, which was on the right side of the new house, collapsed the year after we started living there. When it was cleared, no one got any treasure but only a few stone nagas. They were taken over to the temple and placed there. The wall remained, and was still there on the day I bid goodbye to that place forever.

Father used to visit the property occasionally, sit on the stone steps of the gatehouse and touch those walls. Grandma used to come once a month. It was generally for something court related. When she came she stayed overnight. A few times, she gave in to my mother's pleading and stayed for a week. Mother enjoyed Grandma's visits. A lot of preparation had to be done before each of her visits. Grandma did not use soap. You had to cut and dry *enjapatta* for her. Mature coconuts had to be plucked from the right coconut trees and coconut oil extracted from them. You had to add herbs to the fresh oil, and then boil it with a pinch of pepper. That was for her hair. For her body, the coconut oil had to be boiled with saffron. We also had to procure herbs for her to brush her teeth with. That came from Triparrappu. Arrangements had to be made for fresh vegetables to be delivered in the morning and fresh fish in the evening. She was very particular about everything. The rice grain had to be three years old, the tamarind two years, the palm sugar one year, the coconuts one month, the spinach one week and the buttermilk one day. In the evenings, Thankamma Nadathi would bring fresh palm toddy. When Grandma drank her fill of it with occasional bites of fried fish, she relaxed. Grandma never cuddled kids. This was the only time we could touch her.

There was a spacious yard at the back of the house where there was a stove for boiling grains, a shed for storing coconuts and another for firewood. The streaming moonlight and the shadow of two large mango trees used to create artistic patterns on the cemented yard. Grandma liked to sit there listening to the flapping of the palm leaves. The first one to approach her would be my younger sister. She was named after Grandma – Vijayalakshmi. When she grunted 'hmm' I would join them. My elder brother only came if he was called. I was curious about Grandma's plump hands that showed below her sleeves and wanted to touch them. Her arms and shoulders were covered in tattoos. I once heard Mother say that her breasts were also covered in tattoos. I imagined the valley between her ample breasts to be covered in tattoos too, like the moonlit shadows of a leafy flowering vine on the ground.

Grandmother would sit still, staring at the darkness. We children would ask her, 'What are you looking at?'

'I am looking at death! Life is only that much!' She would sigh.

Very rarely, she told us stories – stories of yakshis – of dark undergrowths, of palm trees, their heads whirling in the wind, of fanged yakshis with cackling laughter who lived atop them, dark ones. She told us of their endless thirst, their lust-soaked rage, their rage-soaked beauty, their beauty-soaked coldness. The body of a yakshi is as cold as the trunk of a banana tree. She is cold and silent, like the waters of the moss-covered temple tank. Amma would sit at the kitchen door and listen to Grandma's stories. In the shadows, the yakshis came alive. Their faces gleamed in the darkness before melting away. In the night, while sleeping, you sensed their presence beyond the wall.

What did my mother really think about Grandmother? I could never fathom that. She never spoke lovingly about her mother-in-law. In front of her friends, she would speak mockingly of her. She would imitate Grandma's look and her speech, and her friends would laugh their heads off. Amma was artistic. She both wrote and painted. Once her husband left for office, her friends would start arriving one by one. One thing I noticed was that women belonging to the carpenter caste were talented and were interested in literature and other arts. Nair women generally lacked imagination. Amma read aloud the Bengali novels that were serialized in the magazines. She read with appropriate inflections of tone and emotion. She cut the pages out of the magazines, added pictures of her own to them and made them into books.

The women brought their children along with them. The children ran amok in the house, but only till Father returned. Silence descended on the house at five. The cows recognized his footsteps on the steps of the river and would moo. The dog ran up to the jetty to escort him home. Father walked noisily, dragging his sandals. The moment I saw him I would withdraw. He insisted that a vessel of water and a towel should be ready for him by the steps of the house; Mother should be waiting for him, silently, behind the door. He would wash his face, hands and feet, then gargle with the water and spit it out loudly. Then he would change his clothes, draw forward his easy chair and relax on it, fanning himself with a handheld palm fan. He wanted a cup of tea, but expected Amma to ask every day if she could bring him tea. She had to ask him thrice. The first two times he would ignore her. The third time he would grunt. He drank tea in small sips, fanning himself in between the sips. After his tea, he would go around the house and the lands, almost as though he was making sure that they were all in place. Then he'd go into the barn and pet the cows. In the night, he had gruel. He had it sitting on his bed. He never made any remarks about the food. If he didn't like something, he would keep it aside. When he did that, my mother's heart would sink.

All the sound he was capable of making was heard once he slept. His loud snoring could be heard up to the river. Sometimes, when he was away from home on official business, Mother couldn't sleep. It was almost as if the harsh sound of his snoring was what kept the house safe. In its absence, even the cows and the dogs grew uneasy.

Though he was mostly silent, once he lost his temper no one could control him. He would beat Mother with anything at hand. His anger would abate and then rise again, and he would rush at her to kick her. Mother did not make a sound, even when she bled or when we children screamed in fear. That is how she defeated him. He would give up, withdraw to the temple veranda or to the riverside and cry.

Father hated and at the same time was frightened of his brothers-in-law, my mother's older brothers. In retrospect, I think he was jealous of them. To her dying day, she was much more impressed by her brothers, who were interested in both literature and politics, than by my father.

The last time Mother went to her own house was when she had my younger sister. After the quarrel between her and her family, father did not allow her to maintain contact with her relatives. She did not have permission to visit her house even when her own father and her older brothers died. For twenty-five years, Mother was confined to the jail built by her husband. When she had enough of it, she killed herself by hanging herself from a beam in the house. When Father returned after checking the cardamom crop one day, he found the house completely locked up. He knocked on the door many times. When he broke open a windowpane and peered inside, he saw her outstretched feet gently moving in the wind.

He stayed alone in that house for fifty days. My sister was in Trivandrum, I was in Kasaragod and my brother was undergoing official training in Madurai. The neighbours reported seeing my father walk endlessly throughout the house all night. They were spooked by the moving light of the torch he carried. After ten days, he went to a shop and came back with tins of paint. He started painting the windows of the house. He spent the whole day painting the windows and spent the whole night wandering through the empty rooms. Before two months were over, he locked up the house securely, threw away the key, went to Cherthala beach, where he drank some poison. The house stood only for another two years. Neither the family nor any tenants were interested in living there. It was demolished and sold for the price of the timber that was recovered. I saw our house for the last time when I went there for my father's funeral rites. A man was busily writing slogans for the AIADMK on the great compound wall.

Grandmother did not like Father beating my mother. Though sometimes she referred to Mother using choice abuses in Tamizh, she could not tolerate anyone speaking ill of her.

'You stupid dog, if she gives one back to you where will you go and die?' she asked once. Father smiled contemptuously and went away.

Mother, hit back? I cannot imagine Mother or Arunmozhi ever hitting a man. There are lines they will never cross. It's almost as though it is genetically encoded in their make-up. Grandma was not like that. She would hit someone without a second thought. I had seen it with my own eyes – it was a sight I'll never forget in my life.

One day, early in the morning, when we opened the front door, Grandma was standing in front of it. She had her leather satchel with her.

She told her son, 'You beggar, that Kurishu Nadar is still hanging on to my plantain field. Come, let's go and rip his heart out.'

Father replied, 'I can't be bothered,' and walked off to the cowshed.

'Fool,' she spat in disgust. She left her bag on the half wall of the veranda and stalked off, swinging her long umbrella. One of Grandma's fields had been leased by Kurishumuttu Nadar. He said he would return it once the bananas were harvested. But by the time the bananas were ripe, he planted cassava. By the time the cassava could be harvested the plantain trees were growing.

'Run, go after her. That old hag will do something stupid.' Mother pushed me. I ran after her.

Grandma walked along the thin ridge separating the fields and reached her field. Kurishu Nadar and his children were tending to the plantain trees.

'Who is that in my field? Get out of there!' Grandma shouted as she walked forward.

'Mother, stop. Let us talk.'

But before Nadar could finish, Grandma had planted her umbrella in the soil and jumped into the field. Nadar's son was standing nearby. Grabbing a full-grown cassava plant, she started to hit him with it. Two men circled her. She kept hitting him. I wet myself out of sheer terror.

'Grandma, Grandma,' I cried out helplessly.

Hearing the commotion, people ran over. Grandma was still attacking the boy. Her jumper was torn. In the melee, she had lost her dhoti and was wearing only the long cloth that is normally worn under the dhoti. She was still clutching half of the cassava plant. Nadar's son was bleeding from the head. She was destroying the young plantain trees around her as though she had lost her mind. Two men were needed just to stop her from doing further damage. For the ensuing court case, Father had to frequent the police station and the courts for the next six months.

When her relationship with her son, our father, deteriorated, she came to see us at school. Generally she came around noon. A man would walk in front of her carrying bunches of bananas and palm sugar. At the door of the school she would shout, 'Isn't anybody here? Chingaraya, boy! Come here!'

'Coming, Ammini, coming.' Chingaraya Nadar, the headmaster, would come running. 'Please sit. Pillai, bring the chair!'

Grandma would sit. The headmaster would stand next to her, his hands crossed deferentially in front of him.

'Why don't you sit? After all, you are a teacher.' Grandma would invite him to sit. Once he sat down, the conversation would start. Chingarayar was a Sanskrit poet, an astrologer and a psychic. She would examine his writings minutely. He belonged to a generation that felt that a poem was excellent if the grammar was perfect.

Once she left, I was sure to get a beating. The forgetful Nadar would only then remember that her grandchildren were studying under him. The headmaster used to go mad when he came across anything I wrote. These days I write in three languages. I have never studied the grammar of any of these languages.

The foodstuff that Grandmother brought was divided equally among all the students. We too got a share, nothing extra. I would beg my elder brother for his share and eat that too. Grandma would look at the three of us from a distance, grunt and nod her head. That meant we were free to go back.

Grandma wanted children of all castes to study. She insisted that liberation was only possible through education. But what really made her happy was the fact that girls were acquiring an education. I often heard her talk proudly and appreciatively about the queen Sethu Lakshmi Bayi, who had built schools for girls.

By the time Grandma sensed that the times were changing, from the various subtle signs around her, she was already past eighty-five. While she was staying with her second son at Nagercoil, she was shocked to see drumstick leaves, banana stem and wild jackfruit being sold for money.

'Dharma is no more; the end of time has come,' Grandma told Ashari[7] Nanu.

It was only the next day that she discovered that in her daughter-in-law's house, the kitchen and the toilet were both inside the house and next to each other. Immediately, she packed her bags and left without drinking so much as a drop of water.

'I can't bear it, my dear Ashari! I, who have seen so many Brahmins who follow strict rules of pollution.'

Grandma was disappointed in her daughter. When she got to know someone new, her fourth statement would invariably be about her daughter. She was proud of my father. 'He can understand any difficult document,' she would claim proudly. Her second son was also 'okay'.

Her daughter, my aunt, was extremely beautiful. She was married to a high-ranking officer in the army. She knew nothing but how to spend money. When her husband retired after his turbulent years in the army, both started selling their inherited properties. By the time their two daughters reached marriageable age, there was nothing left to sell.

Grandma couldn't wrap her head around the idea that men would not come forward to marry eligible girls from reputed families just because they didn't have any money.

'Drumstick leaves and banana stems have takers, not girls!' she complained bitterly to everyone. She was under no delusion. 'These stupid girls are no good.' The elder one's hair had begun to grey when Grandma had a sudden insight. At that time she was praying at a temple. As soon as she returned, she summoned her lawyer and divided all the lands she owned between the two sisters. She summoned marriage brokers, and within a week she took the initiative, single-handedly making all the arrangements to marry off both the girls.

'They take away the girls from our house, and to do that we give them money!' she spat in disgust as the brides took leave of her after their marriage. Grandma felt that in Kali kala, women like her had no place in this world.

When Grandma came a few days after the girls' marriage to discuss something related to land tax, Father stopped her at the door and asked, 'What do you want?' He would not look at her, but kept his eyes focused on the sky.

Grandma's eyes narrowed, her nostrils flared, 'You won't let me enter your house, Thankappa?' Her voice conveyed her suppressed anger.

'You gave everything to them. Go to them,' Father retorted.

Grandma picked up her leather bag. 'I am going there. I plan to die there, not on some road. Whatever Adikeshavan has planned for me, will happen. You show the true nature of a bastard.' She turned and strode off.

'Ammayi!' Mother ran after her.

'You get lost, girl. You are just his servant. Go!' She didn't look back. 'I will never cross this threshold again,' she vowed. 'Send the children over, sometime.'

'Go, go after her. She is an old woman,' Mother cried, looking at me. Grandma was ninety then.

I ran after her. I stopped her at Kuruvikkattu junction and pleaded, 'Please come home.'

'She is a good woman. She has property. Let her leave him and then call me. I'll come. When she stays there as his slave, can I come?' She was adamant. 'You go, son, I won't be moved by your tears. Go home.' Grandma walked on, stopped, turned, and gave me the usual one-rupee coin.

I returned and told Amma that Grandma caught a bullock cart from Kuruvikkattu junction. Those days, from our village, there were only two bus services – one in the morning and one in the evening. Grandma had to walk eight kilometres to reach Thiruvattar.

Eight months passed. It was ten in the morning. We saw Grandmother standing at the gate and ran towards her. Her hair was uncombed and unoiled. Her clothes were soiled and dirty. She looked like a beggar standing there, clutching her leather bag. Mother ran crying towards her and hugged her, crying 'Ammayi.'

'I don't have anyone to look after me, Vishalam. I did not want to die on the streets.' She could barely stand.

'Come inside, Ammayi,' Mother begged.

'Let him invite me inside.' Her voice was firm.

Mother tried everything to persuade her to enter the house. Father was working in the fields. He would only return much later. Grandma could barely stand. When she stood up, blood dripped between her legs and soaked the red laterite soil. The salty tang of blood filled the air. I crossed the stream and ran towards our fields. When I told Father about her, his legs trembled. He was speechless. He threw the spade he was working with and ran home. I ran after him. When we crossed the stream, Father paused. He was breathless. He scooped up a handful of water and drank it. When he reached the temple steps, he slowed down. Grandma was sitting at the gatehouse. Mother was supporting her. When she saw us, Amma came running. 'Please ask her to come inside and lie down. She is the woman who gave birth to you. I don't want any curse to fall on my children.' Father came closer.

'Come inside,' he said, without looking at his mother, and walked on. He disappeared into his room.

For four months the entire house reeked of the smell of blood. The doctors claimed that Grandma's uterus had rotted away and there was nothing that could be done. 'Let her die in peace,' was the consensus. Then we turned to Ayurveda. Every day, Mother would lift Grandma, carry her to the bathroom at the back of the house and bathe her. The water that flowed from the bathroom was red in colour. By morning the dhoti that was tied around Grandma would be soaked in blood and look like bloody entrails. Every morning the sack on which she slept was buried in the backyard. Mother did everything on her own.

We could no longer eat when Mother served us our meals. My younger sister took up the task of cooking. The Ayurvedic doctors succeeded in staunching the bleeding and brought Grandma back to life. It took four months! She started to eat. When she could sit up in bed, she pulled her leather bag towards her, took out the property documents and once again started her work. She needed my help to take down points and make copies.

One day, when Father was getting ready to go to office, she went up to him and asked him to inquire: 'You go and check, Thankappa.'

Our family owned a temple, which formerly was part of Vattapalli Mana. The RSS had taken it over and was running it. Grandma went to court because she couldn't bear the thought of all castes entering the temple. (The court ruling came twenty-five years after Grandma died. It was ruled that the temple belonged to us. But now, no one in the family is interested in taking care of it. It is a fairly large temple for Unnikrishnan!)

Father turned to her and said angrily, 'I have no interest in cases or fights.' He walked off. Grandma said piteously, 'Thankappa, that is my final case.'

Father continued to walk away. Mother ran after him. She caught up with him under the mango tree that grew in the temple yard. She tried to persuade him to help her. 'It is her final case. If she loses, let her lose. But please go and inquire.'

Grandma had reached them. She was in a rage. She screamed at Mother, 'You vile woman from Nattalathu, he's my son! I'm talking about property matters of his mother's. Who are you to interfere? I know your bloody tricks. You pretend to be innocent in front of me and then egg him on behind my back. Move aside ...'

Mother was staring speechlessly at her in shock. Grandma rushed back inside and returned with her leather bag. 'I am going to my daughter's house. I won't stay at your place and die orphaned. I have a house to die in ...' Clutching her bag to her chest, she hurried out. Father looked at Mother, 'See? Don't you realize now? She is pure evil!' he said.

Mother turned to me and said, 'Go and catch her. She is unwell.' I ran after her. She had reached Kuruvikkattu junction and was sitting down on the veranda of Neshayan Nadar's shop, panting. By the time I reached her side she had lain down on the bare floor. Her hair had come undone, her body was bathed in sweat and was cold to the touch. I grabbed her hand and cried, 'Grandma, Grandma!' Her eyes were open, but she was not responding. Nadar opened a bottle of soda, but by then she was already dead. Nadar discovered it the moment he bent over her to give her the soda.

Grandma was cremated on our land next to the stream. Father asked us to put her leather bag on the pyre along with her body.

I heard about the court ruling on the temple only when my elder brother came to tell me about it. We both sat reminiscing about Grandma for a while. Brother had Grandma's nose. 'Nassar's nose, uncle!' Ajithan used to tease his uncle. His son Sharatchandran also had the same nose. That nose was immortal.

That night, Arunmozhi asked about the temple and about Grandmother. The temple was large, with a round, strong inner sanctum made of solid stone. It will stand for another five hundred years. But what will remain of the blood of these matriarchs? Maybe it will get watered down and watered down and until it slowly disappears. What will they know? The memories of the dead also die. Why, even stones break down into sand. This nose alone will get reincarnated and survive for eternity.

I was lying in the dark thinking about something when Arunmozhi turned to me and asked, 'Jeyan, may I ask you something?'

'Of course.'

'Why did you not marry a Malayalee girl?'

I looked carefully at her. In the darkness her eyes gleamed.

5

The *Yakshi*s of Nanjinadu

I

Yakshi[1]

Drop a small ball of cow dung near a rubber tree and pick it up after a week. You will see that the ball is filled with a sphere of fine roots, a single vein of root anchoring it to the soil. The entire ball will be devoured from within by the tree, leaving only a thin, outer shell.

'Son, she is a yakshi,' Narayana anna once told me. 'Not the native type, but the Christian variety, one who wears a *chatta* – a jumper – and *mundu*. She will eat you alive.'

South Travancore was full of yakshis and neelis. If you move eastwards, yakshis are called *eyakki*, or *aekki*, and when a yakshi is worshipped with offerings she is respectfully referred to as Aekkiyamme. She is the goddess who has been part of this soil from the Sangam period. In the *Silappathikaram*, Elango refers to her as the evil-eyed eyakki. In the story, the shepherdess Mathari meets Kannagi for the first time when she comes to pay homage to the eyakki installed outside the city walls of Madurai. Outside the wall there was a row of eyakkis. Minor gods and goddesses had no place within city limits. Within the walls, Manivannan and the three-eyed Shiva reigned supreme!

There is no fixed pooja for a yakshi. If you start offering daily poojas for all the yakshis you wouldn't have time for anything else. A yakshi will be lucky to get a pooja once a month. The usual practice is to worship her once a year. There are forgotten goddesses residing in the forests – mere eyes on stone, burning with rage – who don't even get that. The offering to a yakshi is referred to as *koda*. The word koda (from the Malayalam word *kodukendathu*) means 'that which should be given'. What was given generally was blood – of hens, goats and, very rarely, pigs. When the Vellalars and Nairs slowly acquired cultural sophistication, an offer of red *thechi* (ixora) was considered adequate. Most yakshis have forgotten when they last saw a drop of blood. Then there is the offering of jaggery pongal, turmeric pongal and another strange pongal made with fenugreek. Some yakshis need toddy with it. Some have to have at least a drop of fresh blood too. There are yakshis who refuse to sit quietly till they get a drop of blood from the family that serves them.

A Brahmin will find it difficult to comprehend the concept of koda. Yakshis are not entities who are satisfied with praises in Sanskrit, such as 'You are immensity, the one with a thousand hands, with ten thousand eyes', chanted to the accompaniment of bells. They are like our old matriarchs. They have seen the waxing and waning of many moons. It is this incomprehensibility that is evident in C. Krishnan's translation of Sundaraswami's 'The Story of the Tamarind Tree', where he translated *Ammankoda* as 'Amman's Umbrella'.

The installation of the yakshi in Eruttimoolai, (literally 'the dark corner') was architecturally a simple affair. It was merely one stone placed on top of another. The dark one, Eruttikari, sat on the thickly forested slope where the southern wind flowed incessantly overhead, almost lost amidst the dense, fallen leaves beneath a Kanjira tree (*Nux vomica*). The people of the household and well-born women could not walk that way. In fact, there were more paths that they couldn't walk on than those they could. But the cowherds would nonchalantly pick up her head to crush green mangoes with before eating them. When I went there first with Kuttappan, I was shocked at the sight before me. From the darkness of the forest two eyes gleamed at me! Not even eyes, but a look. Not even a look, but hatred – pure, all-consuming hatred. The hatred bloomed amidst the green foliage like a strange flower. It was hatred that someone felt for someone at some point. Revenge that smoulders and burns stronger than any poison. Something that intense is not going to die. The pyre that burns a body has its limits. But how can the fire that burns on in memory cease burning?

During the month of Aadi, (mid-July to mid-August) the southern forests scream and laugh maniacally like possessed women – arms flailing, long tresses whirling, veins taut. The petrified land lies still, dreaming of cool clouds in the sky. From the forest emerge winds that slowly gather and roll down the hills, transforming into ochre, mud-coloured whirlwinds. Grabbing dry leaves and grass to clothe herself she makes her way to the valleys. In the valleys, ancient gods steeped in silence, smeared with ash, turmeric and *kumkum*, open their eyes. The long-dormant lust for blood quickens in their veins. In front of their eyes – where history bubbles and boils – unknown to them, the blood of time ebbs and flows. From that a mouthful – a mere mouthful of lifeblood – a mouthful of revenge seasoned with fury!

The progeny of Thengummoodu Ammaveedu had the responsibility of giving blood to the dark one. Like water droplets that had fallen on the floor, they were scattered all over – in Trivandrum and Kottayam, Nagercoil, Chennai and Delhi. They congregate once a year and quarrel over family matters. Garbed in red silk, the *viragi* – the priest – walks in front, carrying the things for the pooja. Behind him follow the people of the Thengummoodu family. They walk silently. Their shiny watches, their white skin untouched by the sun and their newly shaven green chins gleam. In the darkness of the forest, when they see the eyes burning with rage, they forget their petty differences and huddle together.

By the time the offering of rice and turmeric, *thechipoovu* (ixora flowers) and puffed rice, tender coconut water and bunches of areca nut flower is made, accompanied by the music from the reed instrument and the single drum, by the time she is worshipped, the eyes of Erruttikattu Neeli assume the expression of a hungry lioness facing her prey. Infused with her spirit, the feet of the priest move in a frenzied dance and his voice becomes hers. The veins on his neck go taut and stand out, his voice takes on the tenor of an axe head being sharpened, the growl of an unknown wild beast.

'You have come? Where else will you go?'

'I'm here in the forest, sitting sleepless in the forest. Where can you go?'

'Where will you go leaving me here?' Laughter breaks out of his throat – the sound of boulders tumbling down – which melts into a rough, heart-breaking cry. 'You have killed me. No rice or water for me. My god! I've been left all alone!'

He screams obscenities in an alien jungle lingo no one knows any longer and beats his chest: 'Barren woman who lives in a crematorium, may you rot forever.'

Like a lamp that spurts into a sudden, strong flame when oil is poured in it, his voice gathers strength. 'Give me blood, give me hot, steaming blood, give me blood.'

The exhausted priest has fallen down on the ground.

He gets up slowly, trying to shake off his exhaustion, and lifts the rusty old sword which is usually kept in the crumbling southern outhouse of the homestead.

'Last time it was Kunjan Pillai, this time let it be Vellappan Pillai.'

'But he has diabetes.'

'How can that be an excuse. All of you are complicit. Moreover, this is an exorcism. The Mother will drain away many things inside you – nightmares and illnesses.'

Vellappan Pillai walks forward and mutely stretches out his right hand.

The priest will nick his thumb with the sword. If you look at the thumb, you will not be able to allow it. Vellappan Pillai shuts his eyes and turns away.

The priest ceremoniously places the sword on the sacrificial stone. For a moment he shuts his eyes in prayer, calls out 'Devi' and lifts the sword. Vellappan's relatives gather around him and hold his arm firmly so he doesn't flinch.

The priest returns the sword to the sacrificial stone and, grabbing Vellappan Pillai's hand, drains his blood on it and on the goddess's head. The face is drawn in *sindoor* on stone for the pooja. Her wide-open mouth drawn in *sindoor* gets a few drops of blood and becomes a bleeding wound – a festering wound that will never heal. The eyes, the nose, mouth – all are festering wounds. And the pitiless eyes – wounds on the face, in the poet Thiruvullavar's words.

II

Bloodsuckers

'As if all the blood that the yakshis here drank wasn't enough, the Christians brought their own yakshis too,' Kolamma, the old woman from the carpenter family, lamented. 'Muruga, I only hope that my eyes close forever, before I see all this.'

Rubber took over our land like the curse of a yakshi. The Christians brought ready cash to buy the lands and the hillocks that no one wanted, that lay forgotten, overgrown with thickets and undergrowth. They brought labourers from outside who cleared the land, dug pits and planted rubber. These men nonchalantly pulled out by the foundation many a yakshi who had terrified the land. I saw with my own eyes the yakshi from Shoola house abandoned by the roadside, platform and all – the same one who used to terrify us when we returned that way in the dead of the night after watching Kathakali performances in Triparrappu. There were people like Keshavan Nair, who, when he sold his land, made arrangements to shift the yakshi living there – the Ayinikara yakshi – to the temple premises of Aattukara Devi.

The leaves of the rubber tree resembled tender mango leaves. The rubber trees thrived. The land darkened. Bird calls disappeared. The sound of the wind in the thickly growing foliage became the sound of the land. The wind in the trees sounded like the scream of flood water rushing down the slope to inundate the land. Hidden in the soil, the roots of the rubber tree proliferated. They drained the lifeblood of the jackfruit and mango trees. The fruit-bearing trees grew enervated, thin and pale. When people cleared their manure pits, they could see the four sides of the pit matted with white roots, like a pile of writhing earthworms. When the grinding stone was moved, one could see the vein-like roots of the rubber tree beneath. Within a day or two of their dropping, any cow dung would be found by the roots of the rubber tree.

'Soon, this yakshi will seek the cow's arse to eat the dung,' complained brother Narayanan.

'Its efficiency is mind-boggling. Earlier this land was infested with yakshis. These days there is only one,' added Madhavan.

Madhavan used to go up the Pechipara hill, buy tapioca cheap and sell it in the plains on a cycle. The tubers that grew in the plains never tasted as good as those from the hills. That special taste was the benediction of the gods of the hills. He used to cycle up the hill at midnight, return with the tubers early in the morning and finish selling them before noon. Ten years ago, while he was cycling up the hill, he saw a woman sitting on the platform under a tree. Dignified-looking, she sat there without a care in the world. A lone woman, looking relaxed at midnight on an empty road. Convinced it was a yakshi, Madhavan went cold.

As he neared her, he saw that her feet touched the ground. She had bathed in the river flowing nearby. Her abundant hair was dripping water. She had full, round breasts and firm shoulders that looked like they had been carved from the golden wood of the jackfruit tree. Madhavan fingered the sacred talisman he wore around his waist and offered a silent prayer to the goddess. Shivering from fear, he pulled out his knife and walked forward. She looked unconcerned. He could have passed her and gone his way. But what if she followed him?

Madhavan cleared his throat and asked, 'Who are you?' The woman turned and muttered some gibberish. He stretched his arm out and touched her with his knife. There was no reaction. Madhavan began to have doubts. Muttering the name of the goddess, he touched her with his fingers. She was cold to the touch, but appeared totally unconcerned by his actions. She sat there engrossed in her own world, muttering words without any meaning. In a flash, Madhavan realized that she had lost her mind. She must belong to some prominent family hereabouts, had broken free and was wandering alone.

He spoke to her gently, trying to prise information out of her about her house and family. It was of no use. When he repeatedly asked her where her house was, she turned eastward, stretching an arm in that direction.

'Come, I will take you home,' Madhavan said. She agreed and started walking with him, unhurriedly. If she saw a flower, she paused to look. If the breeze blew, she paused to feel it. She was like a child who had not grown into an adult mentally. The wind dried her clothes. Her round, heavy breasts swung with her gait. Her thighs, tapering from her waist, streamlined like the strong haunches of a young colt, moved easily. As they walked, Madhavan felt the stirrings of desire in him, and as time passed it became a raging fire.

When they crossed the elephant hill and reached the other side, she pointed a finger and said, 'That's where we live.'

Her voice sounded like the music of the temple bells. He wanted to hug that sound and kiss it.

'There …' He wanted to kiss the finger that pointed.

Intoxicated, Madhavan went with her, not caring where they were headed. He forgot to wonder whether he had ever seen a house in that forest. He floated weightless, like the soft, flying cotton from the silk cotton tree, the foam of a wave, insubstantial as smoke.

When they crossed the boar corner, they could see the spread of the mighty forest in all its glory. It spread as far as the eye could see, clothing the land, reaching to the skies. A forest in the moonlight is the madness of the gods. The fragrance of *thazampoo* – the screwpine flower – filled the air. Its fragrance was special – the further it was, the further it gained in strength. Like music, the intoxication of which intensified with distance. The forest was silent. Not sleeping but dreaming; dreaming a heady dream it had never seen before.

All of a sudden, Madhavan remembered the words of his grandfather. 'Man has a puny life. He can't consume anything massive.' It was only then that he understood the meaning of those words. He was already hooked. The sharp edge of the fishhook was already embedded in his throat. Yet he struggled. Gathering all his mental strength, he willed his legs to turn around and walk back.

He saw the expression in her eyes change. The eyes glowed red, like embers fanned by the wind. She asked, 'What?'

'I am going. I'm just a poor man,' Madhavan said, stepping back.

'Why are you frightened?' Her lips stretched into the guileless smile of a baby.

'My eyes inexorably sought her feet. The feet had bovine hooves,' Madhavan said.

He turned and dashed away, as though in a dream. He reached the path he used to take. He couldn't remember anything that happened after that.

At dawn, the labourers walking to the Ambadi estate came across his prone figure. There were two wolves hovering nearby. They thought he was dead, but fate had other plans. For twenty-five days he had a raging fever. When the fever left him, he could no longer walk.

'Son, you have a benign fate. In my life I have never come across a man who has escaped from *mattuyechi's* hands. Those days, in that forest, on average at least three people died ever year. No one collected their bodies. Who would go? They would be consumed there itself,' observed Keshu Nair.

'You had the blessings of your ancestors. Else you would have merged with the soil and by now would have leeched into the sea,' was Achutan's cryptic remark.

Potti sir turned philosophical. 'That moment, you had a flash of sense. Generally, it is vanity and lust that lead you to the yakshi's bait. Think about it. Beauty itself is deceit. There is an enigma in beauty that is beyond human understanding. There is a call in beauty. But to where? Beauty says "come hither". The still, deep pond has that call. Haven't you noticed how alluring it is! But if you are tempted, that is the end. What about the beauty of the snake?

'Sometime ago, when the attic in the *cheriyaveedu* caught fire, the patriarch of the house pointed to it and said, "Look how beautiful it is!" Clapping his hands, he did a jig. He had lost his mind. He never recovered.

That's why in the olden days when people got something exquisite, they immediately offered it to the gods to be blessed first. Why do you think Marthanda Varma offered pearls and diamonds to the god Adikeshavan? It is not enough to have a head on your shoulders, you have to know how to use it.'

Potti sir insisted that yakshis haunted the house of Thengummoodu Ammaveedu. If you opened one of the disused rooms in that house, along with the smell of darkness and dust and cobwebs you would also get the faint fragrance of the champa (the flower of the plumeria). After a while it would transform into the smell of rotting flesh and old turds. From the darkness would emerge eyes without a body – vendetta, rage burning like a log-less fire. Many who had witnessed that rage had gone mad. Even if you closed all the windows the smell seeped in. A sliver of the odour of the yakshi found its way inside. Trees withered. The people of Thengummoodu died without cause. The women who married into the family miscarried. Foetuses were born before term, with folded hands and heavy bent heads and had no lifeblood in them. The people of Thengummoodu house tried everything. They brought sorcerers and tribal priests, they brought Tamilian priests and Nambudiris from Kerala, and Tanthris. When the patriarch died, all this stopped. The remaining people of the family locked the house and left. For eight long years, the house stayed uninhabited, covered in dust and darkness, even the roof hidden under foliage.

The heirs met at Nagercoil and divided the property. The homestead and the adjoining property were to be shared by eight people. The businessman Kunjumathan ushered all eight of them into a jeep, took them to the Arumana registrar's office, paid them cash and bought the property from them. He fenced the plot and planted rubber trees. Although he tried to tear down the house and sell it, he couldn't find a buyer for it. The roots of the rubber trees sought out the house and embraced it. The walls cracked; the roof listed. Like a tusker who dies on all fours with its tusks spearing the ground, the house collapsed. The stones survived for a few more years. Then everything became rubble. When I first saw the place, I saw a chameleon on a rock, basking in the tender light of the sun that filtered down from between the leaves. With its outstretched neck and bulging eyes, it stood still, gulping air. Its body was the colour of stone. I watched as it started turning green from the shoulder. Only the tip of the tail retained the old colour. It jumped up a rubber tree and disappeared into the foliage. By then even the tip had turned green!

III

Without Light

In the olden days, houses were dark. The verandas with their half walls were dark, and the darkness spread inwards. If one looked inside from the front yard, a house looked like a cool, dark, mountain lake. You could hear sounds of habitation and movement from deep inside; see a sudden flash of white from a passing garment. If you called out 'Sister … Aunty …' many times, someone would slowly emerge from the depths of the darkness. More often than not it would be one of the elderly women. Their sharp question, 'What is it?' reflected their irritation at being woken up. If you entered, you could see the younger women. They flitted around like fish in a pond that hide in the dirt and amongst the roots of the water plants. These women rarely stepped out. The bright light of the outside world dazzled their eyes. They did not look up. Their faces were crimson and they looked breathless. Their legs faltered. Their words struck against the rocks inside them and scattered, leaving only foam. If someone entered their homes unexpectedly, in a moment they would vanish into the depths, like startled fish. Then the whole lake became full of eyes – eyes that did not blink – huge, anxious lake eyes.

I have watched them in the darkness inside. As I watched their voices grew stronger, from moment to moment, and their steps firmer. As a kid, I had emptied my bladder in fear when I saw my aunt Pankajakshi drag the maid Chellamma by her hair to punish her for a mistake she had made. I still remember the fury in Lakshmi's eyes as she raged out of her room, clothes in disarray, hair undone, to argue with my cousin Rajamma. In the darkness, these women grew stronger. As the darkness congealed, they became invincible. When anger filled them, they burst out of the darkness within the house and sought the darkness of the forests. In the forest it is always dark. Sunlight is merely a warm snack for darkness to munch on.

Lakshmi's husbands had abandoned her, not one but two of them. The only one who stayed till the end was Potti, the old man.

'The old man knows, bro, that you cannot do without,' said Narayanan.

The second husband was Divakaran from Parashala. He only stayed for eight months with her. Later he stopped coming. If you sent someone to him, he would send money and a few household essentials with them. Later, they sent the old woman from the carpenter family, Kolamma, to meet him. When she returned,

Kolamma said emphatically, 'Don't wait for him, dear, it's over. He is an innocent young man.' I eavesdropped on the talk around the pond. 'Who will stay when one man becomes two, two become three?' Enigmatic words, only half comprehended. Sniggers. When Potti sir said enigmatically, 'The poison of a beautiful snake is equal to the poison of ten royal snakes.[2] You children cannot understand it,' I saw the smiles slip.

The viper lays eggs in the damp darkness of the undergrowth where the soil is warm and squishy. When the eggs hatch, snakes as thin as the fingers of a newborn infant crawl out and find shelter beneath the dense, fallen leaves. They eat the grubs and white ants that are found abundantly there. In their eagerness to grow, it is said that they don't even sleep. In a fortnight they grow into thick, long snakes and seek their own path. But when they are baby snakes, lurking beneath the dry dead leaves, they are ravenously hungry – mad with hunger. Touch them and they will bite instantly. If bitten, you don't have time. The countdown begins for the man who is bitten and races with the flow of his blood. Though tiny, its poison packs a lethal punch. Maybe they were given such a potent poison because they are tiny – tiny enough for anyone to grind into the soil. Maybe the weak are always bestowed with such a sting. The bigger you grow, the more you have to fear the weak.

When the eggs of the viper hatch you can smell them. Grandmother claimed that the smell resembled the scent of the screwpine flower. The creamy white screwpine flower bloomed only at dawn. When we smelled it at midnight, we knew it was not the screwpine blooming. Grandmother exclaimed, 'Shiva, Shiva! Bhagvati! Narayana! Someone is due to die.' It was believed that once hatched, at least one man would definitely die at the hands of that brood. It was an unbroken law – unavoidable.

The infant snakes that crawl out of their shells long for the comfort of the screwpine flower, with its soft warmth and the scent of the snake egg. They cannot crawl up, but in every brood there will be one who goes against the grain. It will crawl up the tree, seek the unopened bud and crawl inside. When the flower blooms, within its petals that look like tiny golden pleasure boats, you can see a tiny red bud, like the bud of a shoe flower. It is the head of the viper. That one, with its minuscule red flickering tongue, is in repose. It is the one who sought the womb and went back into it – the one who because of it grew enormous and has a poison with the potency to kill an elephant. If it is disturbed, its rage is unfathomable – the tip of a yakshi's tongue that screams to bathe in blood, the single spark that can burn down an entire forest.

Among all the people from the house of Thengummoodu who shifted to Trivandrum, only Shrikandan Pilla and his eldest daughter returned. They bought the huge house that had belonged to Nesharajan, who had shifted to Nagercoil, and started living there. The house had a high compound wall with a wrought-iron gate. Inside were four huge dogs. They had lolling red tongues and prominent prepuce that swung as they walked. Their eyes had a glint I had never seen in other dogs. Narayanan's cryptic remark was: 'Those dogs have the souls of men. That's why they are so ferocious.'

Shrikandan Pilla had retired from some prominent post he had occupied. He was a reticent man – did not talk much. Neither did he have any friends. The people in the town did not know much about him. He subscribed to all the magazines published in Malayalam. His was the only house where the postman came every day. There was a mailbox with an open maw at the gate. Generally, he deposited the post in the mailbox. When we kids deposited 'letters' in the box, Narayanan chided us, 'Boys, don't. Yakshis live there. Your blood will drain away in the night, and when morning comes you will be white and stiff with empty, staring eyes, like dead sardines in ice.' We agonized over how to retrieve those letters.

Shrikandan Pilla's daughter Keshini was extremely beautiful. In retrospect I can say that she had the face of the ethereal goddesses that Raja Ravi Varma painted – faces he modelled on lovely Nair women – round breasts, full hips, tapering hands and legs, smooth, glistening skin, sharp, piercing gaze, red, full lips, wide forehead, curly hair, pearl earrings. It was very difficult to see her because Keshini rarely stepped out of the house. Infrequently, she opened the gate and came out to call someone. Immediately, all conversation in the square in front of the gate would cease. Eyes would freeze in a fixed stare. When the gate clanged shut after she returned, Narayanan would be the first to break the silence. 'An evil enchantress in the shape of a woman burning me from within, oh Lord!'

'Narayana, your fate, probably, is to get beaten to death!' Keshavan mama, the tea shop owner, would chide him.

Narayanan looked like a spider that had been carelessly swept out of the house – an oversized head on a thin, misshapen body. When he sat down it was a medley of thin, stick-like arms and legs. He had large, restless eyes that glinted. He said, 'One can be born as a worm. But when one dies it should be under the feet of Iravat.'

At Keshini's house, some work was always going on. Workers arrived there every morning with damp, freshly washed hair and dark, glistening skin.

'The bull that leaps over the gate dies impaled on a stick,' observed Narayanan.

'Leave it, Narayana,' advised Keshavan mama.

Narayanan was obsessed with Keshini. She haunted his thoughts during the day and his dreams at night. He spoke about her constantly. 'The Shiva linga at Thirparappu is worshipped with ablutions of oil every day. He is all powerful – an unceasing fire.'

Once a month Keshini went to the temple at dusk on *pradosham* – the thirteenth day of the lunar month. Women waited there to catch a glimpse of her. When they saw her, something burned in their eyes. Some women muttered under their breath, others stepped back and suppressed a smile behind their hands. Even little girls knew of her reputation.

When she left, the charwoman of the temple stepped out and exclaimed, 'In her previous birth she must have been half starved. So this birth, the powers that be have sent her to satiate her hunger. For the One sitting above, all this is cosmic fun. Get lost, kids. Go home, lock your doors and go to sleep. If you feel sad, go to the copse of the screwpine flower, pick one and wear it in your tresses. A pinch of screwpine is enough to drive them crazy.'

There was a champak grove across the stream below the mound. Now there are only four or five left, but those days it was thickly vegetated with champak trees, in the middle of which was installed the shrine for Champaka Yakshi. On a stone platform on top of an ancient anthill stood a stone statue, four feet high, its face and breasts eaten away by rain. Around her, gathered by the wind, lay mounds of dried leaves and flowers. The champak trees looked like the planted antlers of a deer, the leaves its ears, the shade beneath a blue-tinged darkness, like scattered eyes. If you stood there for some time, you gagged with the intensity of the smell, your head reeled, your eyes became dull. Yet at night, when the breeze blew its fragrance across the stream, you were mesmerized by it.

If you smell the champak at night, the elders advise that the young must close their eyes and pray to the goddess. You should not open the door, nor should you have impure thoughts or do impure things. Why does the fragrance of the champak evoke impure thoughts? Inside the petals of the champak is a tightly closed centre. The flower is not a flower.

'No one has the guts to open the door of the shrine, said Potti sir. 'I have heard many stories. Many a time I have walked up to the door and hesitated, with my hand on the latch. I have felt a presence on the other side of the door. No sound of breathing, no fragrance, no clearing of the throat – nothing – yet a being that knows my mind. I only have to move the latch, and beyond it is a world of cool breeze, darkness and the intoxication of the champak.

'Some people remove the latch and step out. They have no return. From that moment, their eyes are alight with a strange fever, they recognize no one; on their face they have one frozen expression – the expression carved on stone on the face of the yaksha at the Thiruvattar Temple, the shringara expression that Kathakali exponent Nattalam Trilochan Nair wears when presenting Nala holding the swan. However you tie them, wherever you tie them, at dawn you will find them in the champak grove. In the end, they shackled brother Karunan with an iron chain. On full-moon nights, he went mad trying to break free. Straining against the chains, his chaffed hands and feet developed pus-filled open wounds. His thighs were stained with semen. One full-moon night he passed away; an expression of wonder fixed forever in his wide-open eyes.

'She will never have enough. Can the fire in the sky pour ghee on the soil?' sighed Potti sir, concluding the story. Even after draining every drop of blood, she will not be filled. 'What else? That's all.' He spat out the paan in his mouth and remarked, 'Just as we captured Melekavile Neeli and installed her, we will have to contain this one as well.'

Melekavile Neeli had rampaged through the land as an unquenchable *yagagni* – sacrificial fire. She was captured by a Nambudiri who arrived from North Kerala. People had gone north hoping to invite a patriarch who was a reputed wizard. They found him bedridden. After they importuned him piteously, he agreed to send his grandson, who had just stepped into adulthood. But the boy did not know any spells. He arrived with only a sacred yellow thread that his grandfather had handed over to him after casting his spells on it. At midnight, the boy walked alone to the forest. Beside a stream that curved and glinted like a snake in the moonlight, she stood – her face lowered shyly, with a body that did not know shyness. She invited him to come with her. She led the enchanted boy into her shrine. The trees around the shrine, which were wilted and leafless in the height of summer, had suddenly bloomed. The full moon blazed in the lake. The breeze blew cool and fragrant.

The Nambudiri covertly removed his signet ring from his finger and dropped it into the adjacent well, which was completely dry. He begged her to get it for him. In her eagerness to satisfy her lust, she agreed and slithered down. The moment she went down, the Nambudiri removed the yellow thread from around his waist and tied it across the mouth of the well. The yakshi did not have the power to break it and emerge from the well. The boy pulled out a conch from his waist and blew it. At this signal the natives rushed forward to help him. Together they took a huge rock and placed it over the mouth of the well, covering it forever. Later they built a platform and installed an idol – a shrine for her.

As the young Nambudiri boy was returning with his reward, he heard the yakshi's heart-rending cry, 'Don't tie me with a curse that is eternal.'

'You will have daily poojas and offerings!' he promised, 'You are now a goddess.'

'Who will I talk to?' she lamented.

The Nambudiri planted a banyan tree next to her shrine. 'Now there is someone who will talk to you, day and night, with a thousand tongues.'

'When will I become free? I need a date to keep my hope alive,' she pleaded.

'If I or any descendants born of my blood step on this land, you will be released that day.' The Nambudiri blessed her.

On the way home, before he left the land, he bought a chisel from a carpenter. He cut off his penis with it and he threw it into the river.

I have sat near the shrine where the tongues of the banyan tree incessantly chatter. I have looked at the stone yakshi and have drawn on it a thousand faces. Myriad faces of women I know have washed over that stone, like a river that flows over rocks.

IV

Against Nature

Those days, our village looked like a long-lost crystal black pearl held lovingly in the dark palm of a tribal woman. It was totally surrounded by forests. In a clearing in the forest stood a hundred houses, and in the centre the temple of the all-powerful Lord Shiva. A river flowed by, and a temple of the Devi stood on its banks.

When Raja Marthanda Varma renovated the Thiruvattar temple, people were sent to the forest to search for a jackfruit tree of sufficient girth. Those days, the forests were impenetrable. In the midst of this forest stood a jackfruit tree so big that if eight people held their hands to circle it, they could do so only with difficulty. On it lived a yakshi called Yamini. The moment the master carpenter saw the tree, he immediately understood that a yakshi lived in it.

'That's the reason for its extraordinary growth,' he warned. 'Both the people who cut it and work on it will be doomed.'

However, the supervisor, Ayyappan Marthandan Pilla, was adamant. He felt it would be a loss of face to choose another tree after selecting this one. So a reputed wizard, Theepanja Perumal from Tamil Nadu, was summoned. He performed intensive pooja for eight full days. On the first day, he ritually sacrificed an earthworm, on the second day a chameleon, on the third day a fish, on the fourth day a bird. On the fifth day a goat was sacrificed, on the sixth a buffalo, and on the seventh day a man. On the eighth day, the wizard cut off his own finger to propitiate the yakshi, infused her into a branch of the tree which he planted on the banks of the Thiruvattar river.

When they cut the top branches of the tree, the birds in the tree flew up and circled it, complaining loudly. When they cut the roots, snakes and chameleons rushed out in confusion and took shelter in the undergrowth. When they cut the trunk and rolled it out of the forest to the river, monkeys followed it up to the riverbank, crying piteously. The tree was turned into an idol and brought into the temple. When the god emerged from the trunk, he must have sighed in pain to see the golden wood chips and sawdust scattered around him. Keezhthadom Nambudiri was summoned to install a Shiva linga on the spot where the tree once stood.

A Shiva linga is a seed. The tree is in the north, in faraway Kashi, on the banks of the Ganga. From that epicentre the seeds disperse and are scattered all over India. They are still sprouting, and so are the cities, towns, villages. Henceforth, the Shiva linga and the land on which it stood became the property of the Keezhthadom family. To look after the shrine, they appointed Kundan Pilla.

Kundan Pilla, who ate rice made from one and a half kilos of grain for each meal, came to the forest with a sword and an axe. He cleared the forest, enslaved the forest dwellers, made them work for him and treated them ruthlessly. He killed so many people that legend has it that he watered the plantain trees with blood and fertilized the coconut trees with human bodies. Kundan Pilla was the man who built the big house at

Thengummoodu, and he was the first adhikari (local authority) of the Thengummoodu area.

Over time, Thengummoodu Pillas, who ate rice made from one and a half kilos of grain for each meal, arrived one after another. The village grew and the forest retreated. Other Nair families settled down in the area. Families of Chettiars, carpenters, ironsmiths and masons came. Households and farms grew in number. When the beloved lord, the king himself, rested for a night at the Thengummoodu house, it came to be called Thengummoodu Ammaveedu. The Pillas also graduated to become Thampis. The people of the land feared the people of Thengummoodu, although behind their backs they mocked their corpulent bodies by calling them 'Buffalo Pillais'. It was rumoured that they hoarded gold coins in the basement of the Thengummoodu house. The house itself grew so much over time that it soon resembled a fortress. In front of its massive front yard, palanquins with silk curtains appeared.

It was one of the Thengummoodu Pillais who killed a tribal woman from Eruttikadu by hanging her on the gallows. He had gone riding into the forest when he came across her mountain hut. She was sitting on the threshold, feeding her baby. The sight of her firm, dark breasts aroused him, and he approached her and grabbed her hand. The woman shook him off and ran away to hide in the forest. Enraged at not being able to find her, he started throwing stones at a hive of wild honeybees nearby. When the bees stung the woman's baby, he cried out. The man tracked her using the sound of the baby's cry. When the woman still resisted, he grabbed her baby and threatened to spear him alive if she did not sleep with him. When she relented, he enjoyed her like a wild buffalo entering a forest stream. After he had had his way, he lifted the child and dashed it on the rocks, killing him instantly. Before he returned, he hanged her from the gallows he rigged up there, for the crime of resisting him. Hanging from the gallows, she stared at him. Veins stood out over her entire body, green and throbbing. Before he disappeared from her sight, she drew all the power from the pit of her stomach to her mouth and cursed him. 'Like the eternal hunger of the earth, may you burn with hunger forever.'

When you walk through the forests, you see myriad gods. Gods are born every day. If you place a stone over another stone, it becomes a god. Is the desire to become a god throbbing inside every stone? Like men and women, on top of each other? Are they forever waiting for hands to pick them up to place one on another? What is the infinite impulse behind men who make gods by placing one stone over another? I too long to leave behind at least one god on this earth. Gods happen through men. But it is the gods who decide the muhurtham – the moment when to part the curtains and enter this realm.

These days, the yakshis in the land are all growing bigger. The shrine of Melankottu Yakshi has been renovated with cement and whitewashed with a coat of Asian Paints. The shrine for of the Arulmiku Nadukattu Ishakkiyamman is in the centre of Nagercoil town. The whole town is full of yakshis – Vakayadiyekshi, Ponthakkadu Yakshi, Theradi Eshakki, Kulathadi Eshakki. In the Kakum Perumal compound belonging to cloth traders, there is a Valliamma Yakshi. In a tiny shrine made of limestone stands her small idol carved out of stone, with bright eyes made from silver, a shiny nose pin, and a garland of old flowers. Every new-moon night there is a pooja for Valliamma Yakshi, and once a year she receives a koda. Nagasami Konar, who lives in the compound, has seen her in person.

Valliamma was a famous courtesan who lived near Vadasherri Kanakam Moolam Market. She was the benign one. Even if you gave her a quarter, she would shower more love on you than your wife. If you came without a penny, but with desire burning in you, she would not send you back unsatisfied.

'Man has two hungers. She was blessed because she saw to one,' Valiyakonnar used to say. The rich and the powerful, enraptured by her beauty, tried to lure her away with promises of mansions. She refused to move away from Vadasherri Market. Even in the end, when she was rotting with disease, she remained the favourite elder sister to all the young prostitutes. When Kakumperumal Pillai's father Ananjaperumal Pillai was on his deathbed, he kept calling for her feverishly, 'Valli, Valli.' He couldn't die. For twelve days he hovered on the edge of death. The belief was that if you stayed like that for fourteen days without crossing over, even Lord Mahadeva would not be able to help you enter heaven. The vaidyar – the native doctor – guessed what was wrong and said, 'He is asking for Valliamma.' Valliamma arrived, smiled sweetly at him, lifted his head and pressed it to her bosom. Ananjaperumal Pillai died on her breast, peacefully, with a radiant smile on his face. She did not accept even a single note from the bundle of money that Kakumperumal Pillai offered her. She just accepted the *thamboolam* – the betel leaf and betel nut – and left.

When Valliamma fell ill and became too sick to work, Kakumperumal Pillai gave her one of the row houses he had built as rental property and looked after her. On the day she turned eighty, on a new-moon night, as she was sitting in her front yard, she sighed 'Mother', and with it her breathing stopped forever. Kakumperumal Pillai built her a shrine on that very spot. Today it is a fairly large temple. It is said that when babies fall ill, if you light a *neyvillakku* – a ghee-filled lamp – at the temple, your child will be cured before you return home.

These days, I pass daily by bus the very spot where Neeli used to stand with her newborn, hooking unwary travellers with her request for a smear of lime for her betel leaf. I live and have built a house in the land where Neeli used to exist. Like the pencil tree (*Euphorbia tirucalli*) that begins as one body and proliferates multiple bodies to grow enormous, she was once all-pervasive here. Sometimes I wonder, 'Is she, the yakshi of the Panchavan forest, among the women who get on the bus?' Then I think once again of Keshini; she who would bathe at dawn in the ice-cold water of the pond even in January. The servant Velamma claimed that she smeared herself with crushed red-hot bird-eye chillies and sighed, 'Cursed! What else?'

Keshini bound her hands and feet to her body with long vines and jumped into the pond and committed suicide. People rushed over from all corners to see her.

It was said that in the water she gleamed golden, like a freshly slaughtered and peeled jackfruit tree. Is this slim girl holding a child on her hip, asking me to make space for her to sit in the bus, a yakshi? I wonder. Then I relax. It is very easy to spot a yakshi. She will not hide from a man whose eyes blaze with lust!

Notes

1. Even Though

1. Thunchaththu Ramanujan Ezhuthachan, is a sixteenth century Malayalam devotional poet. He was a linguist and translator, and is revered as the father of the modern Malayalam language.
2. N. Kumaran Asan (1873–1924) is a celebrated Malayalam poet. Known as 'Mahakavi' (great poet) after he was awarded the honorific title in 1922 by the Madras University, Asan was equally influential as a social reformer.
3. Changampuzha Krishna Pillai is a celebrated twentieth-century Malayalam poet. He achieved cult status with his hugely popular poem *Ramanan* (1936).
4. A reference to the eponymous hero in Changampuzha's *Ramanan*.
5. A reference to Thakazhi Sivasankara Pillai's popular novel *Chemmeen* which was made into a blockbuster movie by Ramu Kariat in 1965. It is the story of a Muslim youth who falls in love with a Hindu fisherwoman. The girl is married off by her parents to a Hindu boy. Heartbroken, the pair consummate their love, thereby committing adultery and take their own lives.
6. G. Sankara Kurup, (1901–1978) is popularly known as 'Mahakavi G'. He is considered one of the doyens of Malayalam poetry. His contribution to criticism is also noteworthy.

7. Poonthanam Nambudiri (1547–1640) the author of the masterpiece *Jnanappana*, (*The Song of Divine Wisdom*) reinvented the scope of Malayalam poetry. *Jnanappana* is a devotional poem on the lines of Bhakti poetry. The poem uses simple expressions to convey deep philosophical thought.
8. Vyloppilli Sreedhara Menon (1911–1985) was a renowned Malayalam poet.
9. Vallathol Narayana Menon (1878–1958) was a Malayalam poet. His contribution to the preservation and revitalization of Kathakali is immense. He is the founder of Kerala Kalamandalam.
10. Caste name. Considered lower caste during this period.
11. D. Jayakanthan and Janakiraman are twentieth-century Tamil writers.
12. M.T. Vasudevan Nair (1933 – 2024) is a famous Malayalam author. Apart from fiction, he is also famous for his movie scripts.
13. Edasseri, in his masterpiece *Poothappattu*, tells a magical tale of demoness' love for a child. The poem celebrates the transformative power of maternal love. It is the story of a yakshi who transforms into a divine being who comes down to the village once a year after the harvest, to bless the households.
14. In Vastu, or the traditional science of a building, a kol is a unit of measurement. It is 72 centimetres, or 2.36 feet.
15. *Thidambu* is a god's image, which is carried on the elephant in temple processions.

2. Nanchinadu - The Part of Kerala That Broke Off

1. A respectful way of addressing older women.
2. Traditional Kerala two-piece saree.

3. Traditional, wide-mouthed, shallow vessel used for cooking large quantities of food.
4. An anna was a currency unit formerly used in pre-independent India. It is equal to one-sixteenth of a rupee. It was further subdivided into 4 paise (old) or 12 pies (there were 192 pies in a rupee). The rupee was decimalized in 1955 and subdivided into 100 paise. 1 anna is roughly equivalent to 6.25 paise (new).
5. *Chuckram* was a type of currency issued by the state of Travancore. The Travancore rupee was subdivided into 7 *fanams*. These *fanams* were further subdivided into 4 chakrams, each consisting of 16 kasu.
6. Nair, Vellala, Potti, Kaipalli, Pervattan, Nadar, are all caste names.
7. The kings of Travancore, from Marthanda Varma onwards, offered up their land to Lord Padmanabhaswamy. They considered themselves the vassals or *dasan* of the Lord and ruled the land on His behalf.
8. In the matriarchal system followed by many castes in much of Kerala, property passed through the females and their progeny.
9. C.V. Raman Pillai's magnum opus *Marthandavarma* (written in 1885, published in 1891) is a historical romance novel in Malayalam that recounts the history of Venad (Travancore). The story narrates the events that preceded Marthanda Varma's ascension to the throne. Initially, he was prevented from becoming the king by the powerful feudal lords of eight houses that controlled power in Travancore, *Ettu Veetil Pillamar*. Marthanda Varma defeated them comprehensively and established his rule. The story is a celebration of his bravery.

3. Daughter, Mother, Woman

1. A marakkál is a grain measure which was in use in Madras State of British India. It is 28 lb./12 oz./ 13 dr./22 grams.

4. Signs Left Behind by Ancestors

1. Abbreviated form of Padmanabhapuram Palace, the palace of the kings of Travancore.
2. Sambandham was an informal mode of marriage followed by Nambudiris, Nairs, Kshatriyas and Ambalavasis. Sanctioned by custom, it was an alliance between a man and a woman which permitted them to cohabit as husband and wife for a period of time. Since the lineage is traced through the mother (for Nairs), this permitted men to have brief liaisons without taking the responsibility for their progeny. However, it also gave women enormous power to decide the nature and longevity of their relationships.
3. Kerala, being a largely matriarchal society, lineage is traced through mothers and not through fathers among many castes.
4. Malayalam film hero Prem Nazir.
5. The kings and queens of Travancore reigned in the name of the Lord Padmanabha. So all the laws were considered His laws.
6. According to custom, this action indicated the end of their marriage. The woman had the right to terminate a marriage when she so desired.
7. The word '*ashari*' means carpenter. Here it is used as a reference to his caste.

5. The *Yakshi*s of Nanjinadu

1. Like the banshee in Ireland, a yakshi is a demoness native to Kerala. The word is difficult to translate because English equivalents like 'witch' or 'demoness' fail to capture the nuances of her reality. Yakshis are female, often women who were wronged when they were alive. They reincarnate as a yakshi to wreak vengeance on the people who wronged them. According to legend, a yakshi sit beneath the Pala tree (Also known as Yakshippala, Daiva pala or ezhilam pala; Scientific name: *Euphorbia nivulia*) in the form of a ravishing maiden and will ask the unwary traveller for betel nut and pan. The men mesmerized by her beauty will oblige and end up being brutally murdered. The toddy palm (Borassus flabellifer) is also associated with the yakshi. She can be subdued only through powerful magic, and then she transforms into a goddess or her spirit is nailed to a tree. One of the most malevolent yakshi was Neeli.
2. The Malayalam term for the Asian wolf snake is Rajavembala. Its English equivalent does not capture the horror the native listener feels on hearing this word.

Translator's Acknowledgements

I could not have translated *Uravidangal* if I had not received generous support from my friends and family. I started this venture during the second Covid-19 lockdown in 2021 – one of the few positive things that happened during an impossible time. My classes were conducted online and I had enough time to embark on this project.

Without special friends this book would not exist. Sree, who introduced me to Jeyamohan and who encouraged me to translate it; my daughter Anu, who read the drafts and pointed out infelicities; Atmaraman sir, for answering my doubts and for helping me contact Jeyamohan; my literary agent, Kanishka Gupta, who found me a publisher. Most of all, the author Jeyamohan himself, who picked up my calls every time I reached out to him and who supported me throughout this endeavour. The faith he reposed in me sustained me. I would also like to thank my mother, who introduced me to stories and the puranas and instilled in me an enduring love for reading, and my sisters who happily encouraged me.

Heartfelt thanks are also due to Chiki Sarkar of Juggernaut Books, who took a personal interest in seeing this work published; Wesley D'Souza, for his meticulous copyediting and being a patient *sahridaya* and the entire team at Juggernaut who helped make this book a reality.

A Note on the Author and Translator

B. Jeyamohan (b. 1962), based in Nagercoil, Tamil Nadu, is a pre-eminent writer in modern Tamil literature. His most significant work yet is a twenty-six part roman-fleuve called *Venmurasu* (The White Drum), a serialized reimagination of the Mahabharata. Spanning more than twenty-five thousand pages, it is amongst the longest literary works in the world.

Apart from other landmark novels such as *Vishnupuram* (1997) and *Kotravai* (2005), his body of work includes more than three hundred short stories, many volumes of literary criticism, biographies, travelogues, introductory texts to Indian and Western literature as well as essays on heritage and philosophy. He has received many honours, including the Akilan Memorial Prize for his first novel, and the Katha Samman, the Sanskriti Samman and the Iyal Award (Canada) in later years.

He can be found at https://www.jeyamohan.in/.

Sangeetha Puthiyedath has been working as a faculty at The English and Foreign Languages University, Hyderabad, India, since 2009. She is a creative writer, translator and an active researcher.